Erik Satie at the age of 54

(*By kind permission of Edward Clark*)

ROLLO H. MYERS

Erik Satie

'*Et tout cela m'est advenu*
par la faute de la Musique'

E.S.

DOVER PUBLICATIONS, INC.

New York

This Dover edition, first published in 1968, is an
unabridged and slightly corrected republication of
the work originally published in 1948 by Denis Dobson Ltd. A *List of Illustrations* has been added and
the *Discography*, which was out-of-date, has been
deleted.
This edition is published by special arrangement
with Denis Dobson Ltd., 80 Kensington Church
Street, London, England.

Standard Book Number: 486-21903-8
Library of Congress Catalog Card Number: 68-19175

Manufactured in the United States of America
Dover Publications, Inc.
180 Varick Street
New York, N. Y. 10014

Introduction by the Editor

ERIK SATIE COULD ONLY have been produced in France. For its nurture his talent needed that freedom of opinion and hard intensity of tradition existing side by side as they do in France, antagonistic, inextricable and interdependent. England might have produced Satie but would have starved his talent on a diet of ridicule. Germany would never have been able even to bring him to birth. His case is singular, perhaps unique. It is strange that a musician with so small an output should reach the position Satie once held, that of one of the most widely canvassed musicians in Europe. It was a position based largely upon intellectual snobbery. But this was not the whole reason. The testimony of infinitely greater composers, men such as Ravel, remains as something which although inexplicable to a foreign observer cannot be ignored. What was there in the artistic outlook of this strange Parisian whose *Gymnopédies* were orchestrated by Debussy?

What was there behind the elaborate façade of verbiage that Satie delighted to erect between his music and his hearers? The mere fact that these questions are put in a spirit of curiosity that is still active, means that they are worth answering. And that is the reason for this book. Study of Mr Myers's analysis of Satie's music helps us also to realise what it was that influenced Ravel among the older generation of French composers, 'Les Six' among the younger and, as Mr Myers shows us, a musician of a different calibre from any of these, Igor Stravinsky.

In England, outside a small circle of specialists, Satie is remembered as the composer of the ballet *Parade*. For the rest we here know little about his music. I remember a performance of *Socrate* in Paris and I imagine that I must have heard that strange and haunting work here also. Or am I thinking merely of sessions with it in my study? The memory of these things is very vague. Since Satie's death in 1925 his reputation (as a *pince-sans-rire*) never very strong outside Paris, seems to have vanished like a falling star and his music also appears to have fallen into something perilously near oblivion, certainly in countries other than his own. Mr Rollo Myers has rescued Satie's music from complete oblivion. We shall no longer be able to say that we were not told. The questions I have put above and

5

many others are answered in this book. All that will probably ever be known about Satie's life will be found here. And from Mr Myers's sympathetic and, to me, extremely diverting account we may proceed to his keen analysis of motives and technique in Satie's music.

Exacerbated by the footling chatter which, largely through Satie's own fault, produced the fatuous 'legend' and smothered his music, we had gradually ceased to be interested. Mr Myers has pricked our conscience, aroused our curiosity and convinced us of the reality of Satie's position in the history of music.

SCOTT GODDARD

Contents

Author's Preface   11

PART I: THE LIFE

I   Early youth and early influences (1866-1890)   13

II   The Rosicrucian adventure—Montmartre—Relations with Debussy (1890-1898)   21

III   Life at Arcueil—Exploration and discoveries—The Schola Cantorum—First public recognition—The 'humoristic' period (1898-1914)   36

IV   The War years and fame—Collaboration with Cocteau and Diaghilev—*Parade*—'Les Six'—Death of Debussy—*Socrate* (1914-1918)   48

V   'Musique d'ameublement'—The ballets—*Mercure* and *Relâche* — The Ecole d'Arcueil — Last days (1919-1925)   59

PART II: THE WORKS

VI   The Piano Music   67

VII   The Songs   93

VIII   The Stage Works—Ballets   99

PART III: THE MAN

IX   His Writings   109

X   His Character   123

XI   The significance of Satie in Contemporary Music   127

Appendices   131

Index   147

Acknowledgments

THIS BOOK COULD HARDLY have been written without the help of Monsieur P. Templier's biographical study of the composer (Paris, Editions Riéder) which I had to consult frequently for dates and general documentation.

I am also deeply indebted to Monsieur Roland-Manuel who was not only good enough to place his valuable collection of MSS, both literary and musical, at my disposal but also supplied me with a great deal of hitherto unpublished material of a more personal nature derived from his own recollections of Satie. I cannot sufficiently thank him for all his help and encouragement.

I am grateful, too, to Monsieur Paul Rouart (Editions Salabert) and Messrs. Schott & Co. (Editions Max Eschig) for their permission to quote from the music of which they are the publishers; and to Monsieur Rouart especially for presenting me with a rare copy of Satie's ephemeral publication *Le Cartulaire* (reproduced on p. 26).

Finally I would like to thank Dr Robert le Masle for all his friendly assistance and advice, and Messieurs Henri Sauguet and Henri Borgeaud for very kindly placing at my disposal their collection of articles published by Satie in various literary Reviews long since extinct.

R. H. M.

London, October 1947

List of Illustrations

Erik Satie at the age of 54   *Frontispiece*

FACING PAGE

Original manuscript of *Véritables Préludes Flasques*   13

Suzanne Valadon. Sketch by Erik Satie   32

'The Velvet Gentleman'   33

Satie's lodging at Arcueil   33

Erik Satie, by Francis Picabia   64

Erik Satie, by Jean Cocteau   65

Page from the scenario of *Uspud*   100

Portrait of Satie as a young man by Suzanne Valadon   101

Picasso's designs for *Mercure*   106

Frontispiece to *Relâche*   107

A typical Satie letter-card   124

Erik Satie   125

Satie's drawing of a bust of himself   125

Author's Preface

I BELIEVE THIS BOOK TO be the first extended study in English of one of the strangest personalities in the whole history of music. Stranger still is the fact that, in spite of the absolute uniqueness of Satie, both as a man and a musician, to the vast majority of people in this country, including musicians, he is still little more than a name—a name, moreover, which if mentioned at all, is usually pronounced with either a sneer or an air of amused condescension. As to his music, of even the few score or so of musicians who may have a nodding acquaintance with it probably only a very few have ever paused to consider whether the composer was anything more than a musical humorist with a marked penchant for leg-pulling. And that he should have chosen the sacred medium of music as a vehicle for his wit seemed to our pundits, missing the point completely, the most damning thing about the whole affair. In consequence the name of Satie, in so far as it is known at all in England, has come to be associated with a kind of musical buffoonery and with nothing else.

I hope in these pages to be able to convince even the most sceptical that the true significance of Satie is to be sought on a very much higher level than certain of his works might suggest, and that his importance as a pioneer in contemporary music in general, and the influence he has had upon some of the greatest composers of the century in particular are far greater than is generally supposed.

The neglect and oblivion by which his music has been shrouded are, I venture to suggest, unjustified; and if the picture of the man and his *œuvre* which I have tried to paint in the pages which follow can help to disperse the fog of prejudice and misunderstanding by which they have been for too long obscured, my principal object will have been achieved.

Original MS.

(Reproduced by kind permission of M. Roland-Manuel)

Part One: The Life

Chapter I

Early youth and early influences (1866-1890)

STUDENTS OF HEREDITY WILL doubtless note with satisfaction that the improbable career of France's most improbable composer was matched by an equally improbable ancestry. And a certain Captain Satie, an officer in Napoleon's Navy, would certainly have deemed it improbable, to say the least, if anyone had predicted to him that his great-grandson would be, not only a musician, but one of the most-discussed composers of the twentieth century. And if his informant had added that this great-grandson would have a Scotswoman for a mother and bear an English Christian name, his amazement, and probably his indignation, would have known no bounds. For Capitaine de Vaisseau Satie had spent a large part of his life fighting the English, and in consequence was a confirmed anglophobe.

His son Jules maintained the family's connection with the sea, though less actively, having adopted the profession of ships' broker in the little seaside town of Honfleur on the Normandy coast where he was a much respected member of the community. He wore in his buttonhole the ribbon of the Légion d'Honneur, and among his other civic duties he was proud to be captain of the local Fire Brigade.

Jules Satie in due course married an Alsatian woman by whom he had three children—a girl, Marguerite, and two boys, Alfred and Adrien. Both were students for a short time at the Collège d'Honfleur, and in due course were sent to England where they were received into a country clergyman's family. The brothers had very different characters. Alfred was studious and steady, while Adrien was just the opposite. Wild and un-

13

disciplined, he had been given the nickname of 'Sea-Bird', and it is to be feared that his behaviour while under the English parson's roof scandalised the village.

Eventually both sons were set up by their father in his own line of business as ships' brokers in their native town of Honfleur. 'Sea-Bird' neglected his duties and developed into an eccentric; Alfred, on the other hand, settled down and applied himself with exemplary zeal to his profession. Marriage was clearly the next step, and it was not long before he found himself a wife. The girl of his choice was born in London of Scottish parents; her name was Jane Leslie Anton. Her mother (who was lady's-maid to her own sister, a certain Mrs MacCombay) decided, as Jane was growing up, to send her to France to learn the language, and a family was found in Honfleur willing to take Jane 'en pension'. There in due course she made the acquaintance of young Alfred Satie, and it was not long before they decided to get married. The honeymoon was spent in Jane's native country, Scotland, and soon after their return to Honfleur, on May 17th, 1866, a son was born to them who received the baptismal names of Erik Alfred Leslie. Erik's sister, Olga, was born the following year, and his brother Conrad two years after that. Although the Satie family were Catholics, Alfred's three children were all baptised in the Anglican Church. Later on, however, Erik was re-baptised as a Roman Catholic by order of his grandparents in whose care he had been placed after his mother's death. This took place in 1872, when Erik (or 'Crin-Crin' as he was called in the family) was only six years old.

At the time of Jane Satie's death the family was already settled in Paris, Alfred having sold his business at Honfleur after the Prussian war. He decided to send Erik back to Honfleur to live with his grandparents, and entered him at the Collège d'Honfleur where the six-year-old boy then began to go to school.

These early years at Honfleur undoubtedly played an important part in the formation of Erik's character. There were two main influences. In the first place there was his uncle Adrien ('Sea-Bird') by whose odd character the boy felt instinctively attracted; and then there was Vinot, the organist of St. Catherine's, who gave Erik his first piano lessons. Here we have in embryo the two fundamental aspects of Satie's character—his love for music, and his irrepressible irreverence and deep-rooted hatred of convention in all its forms. It would have been strange, too, if as a native of Honfleur he had not been gifted with his share of that pawky Norman humour (the French call it 'pince-sans-rire') of which his fellow-citizen, the famous humorist Alphonse Allais, is one of the best-known exponents.

We know little about Jane Satie's character, but it is at least permissible to suppose that the union of Norman and Scots blood in Satie's parents may well account for certain of his peculiarities. That there was already an odd streak in the Saties is demonstrated in the character of the extraordinary 'Sea-Bird', from whom, far more than from his respectable bourgeois father, Erik obviously inherited the eccentric side of his nature. And the fact that he was instinctively drawn to his uncle Adrien is proof that already he carried within him the seeds of that peculiar and enigmatic personality into which he was later to develop.

A sense of irresponsible, purely arbitrary fantasy can be discerned in the eccentricities of the uncle of exactly the same kind that was to appear later in the nephew. Thus we are told that 'Sea-Bird', whose passion was ships and horses, amused himself by constructing a magnificent carriage superbly decorated—so magnificent indeed that no one ever dared get into it for fear of spoiling the paint. This recalls the famous staircase invented by Satie and illustrated musically in his 'Marche du Grand Escalier'[1]—'It's a big staircase, a very big one. It has more than a thousand steps, all made of ivory. It is very beautiful. Nobody dare use it for fear of spoiling it. The King himself has never used it. When he leaves his room, he jumps out of the window. Consequently, he often says: I am so fond of this staircase that I'm going to have it stuffed. Don't you think he is right?'

Another of 'Sea-Bird's' fantasies took the form of a very handsome boat whose principal attraction was that it served no useful purpose whatever. The boat, which was most elaborately fitted up, was called ' The Wave', and in it the old man would occasionally sit and smoke a pipe. It hardly ever left the harbour, and when it did was manned by a solitary sailor rejoicing in the soubriquet of 'Mâchoire d'Âne' (Ass's Jaw). On the rare occasions when it did put to sea, it would only be to take 'Sea-Bird' and his 'crew' for a short promenade and would then be brought back to its anchorage for a further long spell of inactivity.

It was during this period at Honfleur, when Satie was about ten years old, that he had his first introduction to music. His instructor was the organist of the Church of St. Catherine, a man named Vinot, who had been a pupil of Niedermeyer, Gabriel

[1]From *Enfantillages Pittoresques* (1913).

Fauré's old master. Vinot taught him the piano, and it seems probable that he may also have initiated his young pupil into the mysteries and beauties of Gregorian Plainsong—which, as we shall see, was to exercise a profound influence on Satie's style in later years. As to whether the boy showed any special proficiency at that early age it is impossible to say; but it seems unlikely. Nevertheless the lessons with Vinot certainly contributed something to his musical formation, and are perhaps the explanation of his early preoccupation with the mystical aspects of the art. This was to manifest itself later in the first compositions.

The Honfleur period came to an end when Erik was twelve years old; and in 1878 he rejoined his father in Paris. The following year Alfred Satie married his second wife, a certain Mlle Eugénie Barnetsche. She was an earnest young woman who gave piano lessons and had been a pupil of the famous organist Félix Guilmant. Her stepson took a cordial dislike to her, and refused from the first to respond to her efforts to guide his steps in what she considered the right musical paths. Both his father and his stepmother undoubtedly wished to encourage the boy's musical inclinations, but set about it the wrong way—wrong, at any rate, for Erik Satie. He was dragged to concerts of boring music, and expected to admire everything that seemed to him intolerably academic and lacking in real interest. This was not at all the kind of musical atmosphere which the young Satie was likely to find congenial, and he revolted instinctively against it. Like his uncle Adrien, he was a born rebel, defying society and its conventions and unwilling to be led. Already he had his own ideas about music, and it might have been foreseen that he would never be a model pupil. Nevertheless he was sent to the Paris Conservatoire in 1879, when he was thirteen, and not unnaturally failed to impress any of his teachers there. All his life he was haunted by unpleasant memories of that 'vast uncomfortable building' which he compared to a 'gaol devoid of any attractive features, either inside or out'. He studied harmony with Taudou and the piano with Mathias; and afterwards declared, characteristically, that his harmony professor thought he had a gift for the piano, while his piano professor considered he might be talented as a composer . . .

Be that as it may, it is certain that he passed through the Conservatoire without producing any impression except that of a quite insignificant and unpromising pupil. But he was not wasting his time in other respects. During these years he became a voracious reader and discovered among other authors one who

16

was to be his favourite for the rest of his life—Hans Andersen. This is an interesting illustration of the attraction of 'like to like' and gives us a valuable insight into Satie's mentality. For the similarity of outlook between these two artists can hardly escape unnoticed. Both had the uncanny clairvoyance of a child enabling them to see through shams and pretences—not to say pretentiousness—of all kinds; both possessed the gift of being able to express profound truths disguised in the simplest language. For example the child in the story of 'The Emperor's New Clothes' symbolises to perfection the whole significance of Satie's art—its uncompromising intransigeance and dislike of shams, its perfect candour and single-mindedness.

Indeed, Satie might well have been that child in a former incarnation; certainly it is impossible to imagine him having acted otherwise had he been present on that famous Andersenian occasion. For whatever else he may have been, he could never be a dupe; and throughout his strange and lonely career, surrounded by enemies, rivals and sycophants, who flourished in the feverish atmosphere of the cliques and cabals of the Parisian musical world, he never for one moment allowed his vision to be clouded or himself to be diverted from the path he had chosen to tread. At the same time he preserved his own essential 'innocence' until the end. And so, significantly, when he lay dying the only book you would have found by his bedside, with the exception of the works of Raymond Radiguet, would have been a volume of Hans Andersen's *Tales*.

We must return now from this digression to chronicle what must have been an important event in his life at the time, the publication of his first compositions for the piano. These appeared in 1887, but had actually been composed two years earlier. They consisted of two modest pieces entitled *Valse-Ballet* and *Fantaisie-Valse*, and made their first appearance in a publication called *Musique des Familles*—labelled, characteristically, 'Op. 62'! They were described by the publisher as the work of 'a very young musician' and as being 'elegantly turned out' and marked by a 'graceful rhythm'. The publisher's note goes on to remark that 'all the compositions of this young man reveal a "penchant à la rêverie" and a tendency to avoid rhythmic symmetry'. Already . . .

The piano pieces were followed by three settings of poems by Satie's friend J. P. Contamine de Latour, entitled 'Les Anges', 'Les Fleurs', 'Sylvie'. These were published by Alfred Satie, who was now established as a publisher in a small way on the

17

Boulevard Magenta where he also kept a stationer's shop. The following is a specimen of the rather lame verses by which the young Satie was inspired:

> *J'ai vu décliner comme un songe*
> *Cruel mensonge*
> *Tout mon bonheur.*
> *Au lieu de la douce espérance*
> *J'ai la souffrance*
> *Et la douleur . . . . etc.*

But although Contamine de Latour may not have been a great poet, he undoubtedly had a marked influence on Satie at this period. He was of Spanish origin and inclined to mysticism. And so we find Satie, in his turn, beginning to adopt a semi-mystical outlook, which was none the less leavened with more than a grain of irony—as if he were smiling at his own naivety. It was at this time, owing to his adoption of an air of great humility, that he was first nicknamed 'Monsieur Le Pauvre', and a large part of his time was spent in silent contemplation in Notre Dame. Simultaneously he began to immerse himself in the study of Gregorian Plainsong, and would spend hours in the Bibliothèque Nationale reading books about Gothic art. The result of this new orientation can be seen in the four piano pieces published in 1886 under the strange title of *Ogives*, which were presumably an attempt to convey a 'Gothic' atmosphere in sound.

The same year saw Satie in the uniform of the 33rd Infantry Regiment doing his military service in barracks at Arras. He soon tired of this form of existence, however, and managed to get invalided out of the Army by exposing his chest to the night air (in winter) and thus bringing on a bad attack of bronchitis. During his convalescence he read Flaubert, and discovered the works of an extraordinary personage, Joseph Péladan, who was the high priest of both the Wagnerian cult in France at that time, and also of the Rosicrucian Sect which he succeeded in reviving with all the appropriate medieval flummery with which it used to be surrounded. Péladan took the title of 'Sâr', and the sect became known as the 'Rose + Croix'. The relations of Satie with this strange organisation and its intriguing High Priest will be more fully dealt with in the following chapter, as they mark a very important stage in the evolution of Satie the composer.

In the meantime the year 1887 saw the publication of the three exquisite *Gymnopédies* and the three remarkable

18

Sarabandes, the first works of Satie which were to reveal his genius. Indeed they made musical history, because it is on these works that his reputation as a harmonic innovator and a 'fore-runner' of the music to come principally rests. A few critics have attempted to minimise the claims made for Satie in this connection, but the highest authorities seem to agree that in these pieces Satie anticipated the harmonic language which was later to be adopted and developed by Debussy and Ravel.

Thus the eminent composer and critic Charles Koechlin speaks of '. . . the *Sarabandes* with their remarkable resolutions of chords of the ninth which anticipated by fourteen years not only those practised by Debussy but also the "parallel chords" which were considered so daring when Alfred Bruneau introduced them in the score of his opera *Le Rêve*.'

And a most emphatic tribute to 'Satie the precursor' is paid by Darius Milhaud, who asserts that each work of Satie's has foretold the lines on which French music of the last fifty years was going to develop. Thus, he says, 'developments since 1900 owe the same debt to the *Gymnopédies* as those since 1920 owe to *Parade*'.

Or, as Georges Auric puts it: 'always written without reference to the prevailing taste and style of the day and its fashions, Satie's works have, in reality, *anticipated* those tastes and styles and fashions with the most astonishing precision. Debussy and Ravel in turn understood the significant, incomparable and substantial novelty of the *Gymnopédies* and the *Sarabandes* . . .' So much so that while Debussy paid Satie the compliment of orchestrating two of the *Gymnopédies*, (the 1st and 3rd) Ravel was never tired of telling the older man how much he owed to him, and was responsible for introducing some of his lesser-known works to the select audiences of the Paris 'Société Nationale'. In a characteristic letter to his brother, dated January 14, 1911, Satie makes the following amusing comment on Ravel's attitude: 'Ravel est un Prix de Rome[2] d'un très grand talent. Un Debussy plus épatant. Il me certifie—toutes les fois que je le rencontre—qu'il me doit beaucoup. Moi, je veux bien . . .'

There seems, then, to be a consensus of opinion that Satie as far back as 1887 anticipated some of the harmonic processes which were later to become part of the stock-in-trade of the 'modern' French school, starting with Debussy. And, as will be

[2]In 1901 he obtained a second Prize; in 1905, after having composed *Schéhérazade*, *Jeux d'Eau* and the Quartet, he was not even accepted for the competition—which caused a major scandal.

seen from the opinions quoted above, he is also credited with being a pioneer in a very much wider sense and with having given a 'directive' to the whole trend of music in France since 1900. A fuller consideration of all these questions, including an inquiry into the extent of his influence upon nearly all the great composers of our time, will be found in a la⸀ ⸀r chapter. It is time now to turn to one of the most curious and, in a sense, important phases in Satie's life, the period of his association with 'Sâr' Péladan and the 'Rose + Croix'.

Chapter II

The Rosicrucian adventure; Montmartre; relations with Debussy
(1890-1898)

For what we do presage is riot in grosse,
For we are brethren of the Rosie Crosse;
We have the Mason Word and second sight,
Things for to come we can foretell aright.[3]

WHAT IS NOW KNOWN as 'Rosicrucianism', the articles of faith which the Society of Rosicrucians, or 'Rosenkreuzer' as they were called, professed to believe, seems to have had its origin in the 17th century. The members of the sect were moral and religious reformers who were inclined to impart to their teaching a flavour of occultism thereby creating the impression that they held the key to certain mysteries. They seem to have had some influence on the later developments of Freemasonry, although the two confraternities never merged. There is no evidence that the Rosicrucians ever possessed a central office, or were organised into a Society having officers and a hierarchy of its own. Their bonds were far looser than those of the Freemasons, and the members consisted chiefly of individuals holding the same ideas. The movement seems to have originated in Germany and to have had at first a Lutheran and anti-Roman Catholic bias. Attempts have been made to ascribe the origin of the Society to a certain Christian called Rosenkreuz who was alleged to have visited the East in the 15th century and to have

---

[3]From 'The Muses' Threnodie' by H. Adamson, (Perth, 1638). Quoted in article on Rosicrucianism in Encycl. Brit. to which the author is indebted.

brought back a body of mystical knowledge on which the Society was founded. This, however, is considered to be a purely mythical explanation of the origin of the sect, of which there are no authentic records prior to the beginning of the 17th century. Of the modern societies which have been formed for the study of Rosicrucianism, the most important in existence today is said to be the 'Societas Rosicruciana in Anglia', whose headquarters are in London.

But for the moment we are more interested in the organisation set up in Paris during the 'nineties by Joseph Péladan, author of such works as *Le Vice Suprême* and *l'Androgyne*, and self-appointed High Priest, or 'Sâr', of the 'Rose + Croix du Temple et du Graal'.

As we have seen, Satie had become acquainted with the writings of this personage during his convalescence after leaving the Army in 1886; but it was not until some four years later that he met Péladan in the flesh. And, somewhat paradoxically, it was during Satie's Montmartre period, while he was playing as 'second pianist' at the famous 'Chat Noir' cabaret run by the notorious Rudolf Salis, that he seems to have come under the 'High Priest's' influence; or could it be that he welcomed the opportunity of breathing a more rarefied atmosphere at just that particular moment of his life when the future may have seemed to him not only uncertain but discouraging? At all events Péladan seems to have discerned possibilities in the young Bohemian cabaret pianist, because it was not long before he offered him the post of official composer to the Rose + Croix organisation—an offer which Satie was delighted to accept. The chief compositions dating from this period are the incidental music (3 Preludes) written for Péladan's play *Le Fils des Etoiles* (1891) produced at the Galérie Durand-Ruel on 17th March 1892; and the *Trois Sonneries de la Rose Croix* (1892).

These are not among the most successful of Satie's compositions, but they are none the less highly interesting and have a definite place in his *œuvre* which can on no account be ignored. The music of this period was decorative, static, and relied for its effect upon a certain hypnotic quality induced by repetition and the use of harmonies if not derived from, at least evocative of, Plainsong with which, as we have seen, the composer seems to have been obsessed during his early years. It has been suggested by one critic[4] that the reason why Satie, from the first, was attracted to the study of Plainsong may have been that he 'saw in

[4] W. H. Mellers. See his *Studies in Contemporary Music* (Dennis Dobson, 1948).

the impersonality, the aloofness, the remoteness from all subjective dramatic stress of this music qualities which might, with
appropriate modifications, approximate to his own uniquely
lonely mode of utterance'. This seems highly probable, and the
implications of this theory will be examined together with the
works in question in another chapter of this book.[5] We must call
attention here, however, to another aspect of Satie's curious association with the Rose + Croix and 'Chaldaean Confraternity'.
For, according to its founder, the Sâr Péladan, one of the
principal objects of the Sect was somehow to regulate the arts
according to what was alleged to be the Wagnerian aesthetic.
Now Satie, unlike most of his contemporaries, had never been
infected by the Wagnerian virus, and had, indeed, warned his
friend Debussy against the danger from this quarter—notably
when he made his celebrated remark about the need for culti-
vating a truly French school of music—'sans choucroute si possible'. As a matter of fact his main outside influences at this time,
apart from the attraction he felt for the mystical, medieval
notions by which the Rose + Croix movement was inspired,
were anything but Wagnerian; and if there was any one that pre-
dominated it seems to have been his admiration for the painter
Puvis de Chavannes whose theories about floating, indistinct
backgrounds interested him particularly. And the effect of these
theories can be seen in the shifting, strangely indeterminate
successions of more or less unrelated chords which drift across
the pages of the Preludes to *La Porte Héroïque du Ciel* and *Le Fils
des Étoiles*. In spite however of the, one would have thought,
quite obviously un-Wagnerian tendencies displayed in the music
with which his accredited composer was providing him, neither
Joseph Péladan nor anyone else connected with the Group
seems to have noticed any discrepancy between this music and
their own theories. Or perhaps they were satisfied that if not
particularly Wagnerian, it was at least 'mystical' and ritualistic
enough to conform to the requirements of the Order. Péladan
called his play, *Le Fils des Étoiles*, a 'Wagnérie Kaldéenne', and
although Satie's incidental music could, by no stretch of the
imagination, be called 'Wagnerian', it might easily be 'Chaldaean' . . . in the absence of any proof to the contrary. At all
events it apparently satisfied the Sâr who praised its 'admirably
Oriental character'. As to the *Sonneries* or Fanfares, these were
adopted by the Order owing to the 'originality and severity of
their style', for use in all their ceremonies, and an attempt was

[5] See p. 94 [Trois Poèmes d'Amour].

made to prevent their being performed elsewhere except by special permission of the High Priest.

If this situation had been allowed to develop Satie would have been in danger of losing his independence—which he had no intention of doing. He was quite content to make use of the Rose + Croix to facilitate performances of his works, but objected to being identified with all their aims, and was certainly not prepared to conform to their aesthetic theories. Luckily he saw the 'red light' in time, and made his attitude public in an amusing and very characteristic letter, written in pseudo-archaic French which he addressed to the editor of the Parisian paper *Gil Blas*. This letter, which is quoted by M. Templier in his interesting study of Satie[6], was phrased as follows:

Paris le 14 du mois d'Aout de 92.
Monsieur le Rédacteur,
Suis fort surpris que moi,
pauvre homme qu'y n'ay d'autres pensées
que dedans mon Art, soit toujours
poursuivi avec le titre d'initiateur
musical des disciples de monsieur
Joseph Péladan.
Cela me fait grand peine et désagrément
Car s'y dois être l'élève de quiconque,
croys pouvoir dire que ce n'est de nul
autre que de moy; d'autant que croys aussy
que monsieur Péladan, malgré son
savoir étendu point ne saurait faire
de disciples, pas plus en musique que
dessus la peinture ou autre chose.
Donc, ce bon monsieur Josephin Péladan,
pour lequel ay grand respect et déférence,
n'a jamais eu aucune autorité sur
l'indépendance de mon Esthétique; se
trouve vis-à-vis de moy, non mon
maître mais mon collaborateur, ainsy
et de même que mes vieux amys
messieurs J. P. Contamine de Latour
et Albert Tinchant.
Devant par Sainte Marie
mère de notre Seigneur Jésus, Troisième
Personne de la Divine Trinité;
Ay dit, sans haine ny méchante
intention, ce que mon coeur ressent dessus
ce dessein; et fais aussi serment
devant les pères de la Sainte Eglise

[6]*Erik Satie*. Editions Riéder—Paris, 1932.

Catholique, que cette question n'est
nullement noise ni querelle cherchée
à mon amy monsieur Péladan.
Veuillez recevoir, monsieur
le rédacteur, les humbles saluts d'un
pauvre homme quy n'a d'autres
pensées que dedans son Art, et quy est
triste de traiter un sujet sy
pénible pour luy.

ERIK SATIE.[7]

Having thus made his position clear, Satie ceased actively to collaborate with Péladan, but continued to write the same kind of 'mystical' music until about 1895. For, after his secession from the Rose + Croix, in which he seems to have acquired a taste for ritualistic music and quasi-religious forms and ceremonies, he decided to found a 'Church' himself to which he gave the ironically high-sounding title of *L'Eglise Métropolitaine d'Art de Jésus Conducteur*, appointing himself 'Parcier' and 'Maître de Chapelle'. The aim of this organisation was 'to fight against those who have neither convictions nor beliefs, no thoughts in their souls nor principles in their hearts'. Satie printed and distributed pamphlets fulminating against those responsible for 'the moral and aesthetic decadence of our time', and edited a short-lived journal entitled *Le Cartulaire de l'Eglise Métropolitaine d'Art de Jésus Conducteur*.

Giving full rein to his fantasy he establishes a most elaborate hierarchy of dignitaries connected with his 'Church', inventing strange offices and calling for the recruitment of astronomical numbers of hierophants. For instance he would require no less than 1,600,000,000 'Pénéants Noirs Convers', who would be clad in black robes with a grey hood; eight million of another sort of 'Pénéants'; forty thousand of another kind, and so on. The 'arms' of the Church were to be: A large Battle Sword and a Lance five metres long.

The real object of this journal, *Le Cartulaire*, which Satie issued from his Montmartre lodging (on which he conferred the dignified title of 'Notre Abbatiale') seems to have been primarily to provide him with a means of publishing violent diatribes against his enemies and castigating publicly his particular bugbears in the journalistic and artistic world. Chief among these at the time were the actor Lugné-Poë and the critic Gauthier-Villars (better known as 'Willy', the one-time husband of

[7]The English translations of this letter and of those following appear as Appendix A.

CARTVLAIRE

DE L'EGLISE MÉTROPOLITAINE D'ART DE JÉSVS CONDVCTEUR

SVPRÉMATIALES

Eglise Métropolitaine d'Art de Jésus Conducteur.

ABBATIALE, *le 2 du mois de Mai de 1895. Erik Satie, Parcier et Maître de Chapelle, à M. Gauthier-Villars.*

Contre l'enflure de son Esprit et en protection des Choses Magnifiques.

Monsieur; Le caractère sacré de l'Art rend plus délicate la fonction de critique; vous avilissez cette fonction par l'inexcusable irrespect et l'incompétence que vous apportez dans son exercice. Sachez, par Dieu, que toutes les consciences vous réprouvent de vouloir atteindre, pour le ternir, ce qui est au-dessus de vous.

Le démoniaque dragon de la présomption vous aveugle. Vous avez fait un blasphème de votre jugement sur Wagner, qui est pour vous l'Inconnu et l'Infini; pour Moi, Je puis le maudire tranquillement, Mes mélodies dynastiques, Mon expression athlétique et l'ascétisme de Ma vie M'en donnent le pouvoir. Après ces paroles, Je vous ordonne l'éloignement de Ma personne, la tristesse, le silence et une douloureuse méditation.

ERIK SATIE.

Eglise Métropolitaine d'Art de Jésus Conducteur.

ABBATIALE, *le 14 du mois de Mai de 1895. Erik Satie, Parcier et Maître de Chapelle, à M. Gauthier-Villars.*

En expression du mépris attaché à sa personne.

Jaloux des réputations trop hautes pour votre bassesse, les grandes carrières et les triomphes prolongés remuent le fiel dont vous essayez de salir tout ce que vous approchez. J'ai parlé de Wagner et de votre ignorance obscure; vous répondez par d'extravagants accouplements de mots, par ce qu'un écrivain moins louable que loué, Victor Hugo, appelait les excréments de l'esprit. Votre haleine exhale le mensonge, votre bouche répand l'audace et l'impudeur. Votre turpitude s'est retournée contre vous; elle a étalé aux yeux des plus frustes natures votre incomparable grossièreté. Que peuvent dire les esprits sains devant tant d'orgueil mis au service de tant de petitesse? Je ne puis qu'ignorer les infamies d'un bouffon; mais Je dois lever la main pour renverser les oppresseurs de l'Eglise et de l'Art, ceux qui, comme vous, n'ont point connu le respect d'eux-mêmes. Pour ceux-là qui espèrent triompher de Moi par l'injure et la terreur, qu'ils sachent que Je suis résolu et que Je ne redoute rien. Est-ce donc parce que Gauthier-Villars, répugnante « ouvreuse du cirque d'été », faux histrion sous le nom de Willy, seule abjection en trois ignominies, est un sordide mercenaire de la plume, un constant déshonneur parmi les plus vils, que Je n'oserais pas contre lui ce que J'oserais contre le pire malfaiteur? Qu'il se détrompe.

ERIK SATIE.

CONFRÉRIALES

Notre Cher et Vénéré Parcier avait jugé nécessaire de donner à M. Gauthier-Villars (Willy) un avertissement absolument personnel au sujet de sa malhonnête conduite, qui consiste à salir par de déloyales critiques et des trivialités sans nom les efforts de quiconque croit remplir une besogne plus utile que la sienne. M. Gauthier-Villars, habitué à l'insulte, à la mauvaise foi et aux plus fatigants calembours, a reproduit dans une feuille publique des fragments, tronqués à dessein, de la lettre du Parcier, en les accompagnant d'injures injustifiées et dont nul homme bien élevé n'eût osé se servir. M. Gauthier-Villars reçoit ici la juste punition qu'il a encourue.

Note du Définitoire.

Les Chrétiens qui ont à énoncer des revendications d'ordre esthétique touchant M. Lugné-Poë, le théâtre de « l'Œuvre » qu'il dirige, et la presse détestable qui l'inspire et le glorifie, doivent les faire connaître au siège de Notre Abbatiale, 6, rue Cortot. Nos Frères trouveront en Nous un rempart contre les œuvres sataniques, manifestées dans le *Mercure de France*, la *Revue Blanche* et la *Plume*, en même temps que la force nécessaire pour assurer le respect dû à Dieu, à l'Eglise et à l'Art.

ERIK SATIE.

26

Colette) who wrote under the pseudonym of 'L'ouvreuse du Cirque d'Eté'. The latter had apparently incurred the wrath of Satie for having criticised Wagner in offensive terms; and it is characteristic of Satie that, although no Wagnerite himself, he would not tolerate any attempt to belittle Wagner's genius on the part of people whose judgement in other matters he despised. Accordingly he launched an attack on the unfortunate Willy couched in the following terms—(I quote from one of the rare copies still in existence of *Le Cartulaire* dated May 1895):

Eglise Métropolitaine d'Art de Jésus Conducteur.
Abbatiale, le 2 du mois de Mai de 1895. Erik Satie, Parcier et Maître de Chapelle, à M. Gauthier-Villars.
Contre l'enflure de son Esprit et en protection des Choses Magnifiques.
Monsieur: Le caractère sacré de l'Art rend plus délicate la fonction de critique; vous avilissez cette fonction par l'inexcusable irrespect et l'incompétence que vous apportez dans son exercice. Sachez, par Dieu, que toutes les consciences vous réprouvent de vouloir atteindre, pour le ternir, ce qui est au-dessus de vous.
Le démoniaque dragon de la présomption vous aveugle. Vous avez fait un blasphème de votre jugement sur Wagner, qui est pour vous l'Inconnu et l'Infini; pour Moi, Je puis le maudire tranquillement, Mes mélodies dynastiques, Mon expression athlétique et l'ascétisme de Ma vie M'en donnent le pouvoir. Après ces paroles, Je vous ordonne l'éloignement de Ma personne, la tristesse, le silence et une douloureuse méditation.

ERIK SATIE.

This was followed by a second attack in the same place, but dated May 14.

.... à M. Gauthier-Villars
En expression du mépris attaché à sa personne.
Jaloux des réputations trop hautes pour votre bassesse, les grandes carrières et les triomphes prolongés remuent le fiel dont vous essayez de salir tout ce que vous approchez. J'ai parlé de Wagner et de votre ignorance obscure; vous répondez par d'extravagants accouplements de mots, par ce qu'un écrivain moins louable que loué, Victor Hugo, appelait les excréments de l'esprit. Votre haleine exhale le mensonge, votre bouche répand l'audace et l'impudeur. Votre turpitude s'est retournée contre vous; elle a étalé aux yeux des plus frustes natures votre incomparable grossièreté. Que peuvent dire les esprits sains devant tant d'orgueil mis au service de tant de petitesse? Je ne puis qu'ignorer les infamies d'un bouffon; mais Je dois lever la main pour renverser les oppresseurs de l'Eglise et de l'Art, ceux qui, comme vous, n'ont point connu le respect d'eux-mêmes. Pour ceux-là qui espèrent triompher de Moi par l'injure et la terreur, qu'ils sachent que Je suis résolu et que Je ne redoute rien. Est-ce donc parce que Gauthier-

27

Villars' repugnante 'ouvreuse du cirque d'été', faux histrion sous le nom de Willy, seule abjection en trois ignominies, est un sordide mercenaire de la plume, un constant déshonneur parmi les plus vils, que Je n'oserais pas contre lui ce que J'oserais contre le pire malfaiteur? Qu'il se détrompe.

ERIK SATIE.

The author of these violent and extremely personal diatribes was not, apparently, sued for libel; but it is not surprising to learn that on one occasion he and Willy came to blows in a Parisian concert-hall, using fists and walking-sticks. I have thought it worth while to publish these letters for two reasons: for the light they throw on Satie's character—violent, idealistic, proud—and as evidence of his remarkable command of language. Moreover the *Cartulaire* is certainly one of the oddest literary productions in musical history. It soon disappeared from circulation—as soon, in fact, as the small legacy which had enabled Satie to print it was exhausted; and there can be very few copies in existence to-day. All the articles were from his pen, some signed by himself, some appearing over such signatures as: 'François de Paule, Sire des Marches de Savoie', or 'François Marie, Evèque de Séez'. This preoccupation with ecclesiastical things seems with Satie to have been something more than a hobby; all his life he was interested in ritual and ceremonial, and even when later on he became a member of the Socialist party he would never tolerate anything approaching blasphemy, or disrespect towards the Church. Indeed he once issued a political manifesto directed against the anti-clericals—'A bas les Bouffeurs de Curés! à bas les Sans-Culottes! à la porte les voyous! Vive la Calotte! etc'. At the same time there is no evidence that he was definitely religious, although we know he enjoyed the friendship and esteem of serious Catholic thinkers such as Jacques Maritain. At an early age, as we have seen, he was attracted by Gothic art and Gregorian Plainsong which appealed to the 'mystical' side of his nature, and he was evidently amused and intrigued by ecclesiastical terminology. It is highly probable, then, that in founding his 'Church' with the high-sounding name he was to some extent indulging his taste for 'dressing up' and adopting a 'pose' from which he must have derived a good deal of secret amusement, as for example when he referred to himself as 'Notre Cher et Vénéré Parcier' (a term, by the way, he seems to have invented). Nevertheless it is equally clear that he was in deadly earnest about the ultimate aims of his 'Church', which were none other than the defence of art and the 'regeneration of Western society'.

His priestly duties, however, did not prevent him from composing, and the music of this period includes the Four Preludes (1893), the *Prélude à la Porte Héroïque du Ciel* (1894), and the *Messe des Pauvres* (1895). He came also at this time under another influence, that of an esoteric group led by a certain Jules Bois, for whom he composed the *Porte Héroïque* Prelude; while part of his *Messe des Pauvres* was published in the group's Journal, *Le Cœur*, introduced by an enthusiastic article from the pen of his brother Conrad which appeared in the issue for June 1895 and reveals Satie as a disinterested idealist 'professing nothing but disdain for that realism that has obscured the intelligence of his contemporaries. How many persons only cultivate the arts in order to enjoy the goods of this world and to satisfy their vanity! Erik Satie, on the contrary, would rather live with his thoughts in poverty than without them in prosperity; his works are written solely for art's sake'. The writer then quotes a saying of John Stuart Mill's to the effect that what a man writes to earn his daily bread has no life of its own, and goes on to predict that in consequence 'Erik Satie can only expect from the masses to meet with mockery and indifference . . . which has led him to the conclusion that an artist cannot form a school since art cannot be taught'. After referring to the importance attached by the Primitives to prayer and belief in God, the writer quotes Satie as having often expressed the opinion that what the Statutes of Siena laid down for the observance of painters should apply equally to all artists, namely 'to manifest by the grace of God the things that miraculously come to pass through the exercise of Faith'. Then follows an interesting assessment of the *Gymnopédies* and the *Sarabandes* as being the work of a 'pagan mystic' heralding the appearance of the Catholic in the *Danses Gothiques*, and the 'Christian mystic' in the works of the Rose + Croix period including the *Hymne au Drapeau* (from Péladan's *Prince de Byzance*)—'the Hymn of a chosen people acclaiming the immaculate standard of the Absolute'.

Next a reference is made to a work of Satie's that does not seem to have survived, the *Neuvaines pour le plus grand calme et la forte tranquillité de mon âme, mises sous l'invocation de Saint Benoît* described as the 'work of a mystic who must be visited by the Holy Spirit as was St. Benoît during the years when he was known to no man except the holy monk Romain'. Conrad Satie concludes his article with the following analysis of his brother's *Messe des Pauvres* (of which only the *Kyrie* and the *Prière des Orgues* have been preserved). 'It opens with a very characteristic

Prelude which forms the basis of the Mass and consists of "motets" (sic) which recur again and again all through the service and are repeated by the organ and by the choir. Between the *Kyrie* and the *Gloria* a Prayer is interpolated called the *Organs' Prayer*. Through the voices of men and children the faithful implore pity; but it is for the organ to gather up all these cries of distress and convey to the Creator the prayer of the whole assembly. For this Mass is essentially a Catholic work—music for Divine sacrifice—and there is no place in it for those orchestras which figure unhappily in so many Masses. . . . After hearing this Mass one might well repeat what Sainte-Beuve said apropos of Pascal: "On peut rester incrédule, mais il n'est plus permis de railler ni de blasphémer. . . ." '

But in spite of flattering articles of this kind appearing in obscure corners of esoteric and semi-private journals, and in spite of Satie's connection with Péladan and the Rosicrucian sect, it must not be forgotten that he was still almost entirely unknown. And yet it was at this juncture that he made a determined effort to enter the Institute, offering himself in all seriousness as a successor to Gounod, whose death in 1893 had caused a vacancy. His canvassing met with no success however (which was hardly surprising) so he wrote an indignant letter to Saint-Saëns protesting against the humiliation to which he had been exposed, and the outrage done to Art by his exclusion, motivated solely by 'vulgar preferences'.

The tone of the letter, which was published in *Le Ménéstrel* (May 1894) is incredibly haughty and suggests that Satie really thought he had Divine support for his candidature. In it he trounces Saint-Saëns soundly, telling him that he is in danger of hell-fire, and that his 'aberration' can only be due to his 'refusal to accept the ideas of the century', and that his 'ignorance of God' is the immediate cause of such a lowering of aesthetic standards. At the end, however, like an Archbishop giving absolution, he writes: 'Je vous pardonne en Jésus-Christ et vous embrasse en la grâce de Dieu'.

This, by the way, was his second rebuff, as two years earlier he had applied, equally unsuccessfully, for the vacancy created at the Beaux Arts through the death of Debussy's old Conservatoire professor, Ernest Guiraud. On this occasion he accompanied his application by a complete list of his works in which each of the three *Gymnopédies* (which were, of course, short piano pieces) was described as an 'orchestral suite'. On a third occasion he applied unsuccessfully for the chair that became vacant on the death of Ambroise Thomas. In later life, when he was beginning to be better known, Satie published, as a chapter in his *Mémoires d'un Amnésique* the following account of these three unsuccessful attempts to enter the Institut de France, under the title of 'Mes Trois Candidatures'.[8]

More fortunate than myself Gustave Charpentier is now a member of the Institute. Will he accept the affectionate congratulations of an old friend? I was myself a candidate for election to this Delicate Assembly on three occasions: for the succession of Ernest Guiraud, Charles Gounod, and Ambroise Thomas. But MM. Paladilhe, Dubois and Lenepveu were elected, for no good reason, in preference to myself. And that caused me much sorrow.

Although I am not particularly observant, it seemed to me that the Previous Members of the Academy of Fine Arts behaved towards me in a way that revealed a high degree of stubbornness and calculated obstinacy. And that caused me much sorrow.

When M. Paladilhe was elected my friends said to me: 'Never mind; later on he'll vote for you, Maestro, and his support will carry a lot of weight'. I never had his vote, nor his support, nor his weight. And that caused me much sorrow.

When M. Dubois was elected my friends said to me: 'Never mind; later on they will both vote for you, Maestro, and their combined support will carry a lot of weight'. I never had their votes, nor their support, nor their weight. And that caused me much sorrow.

I then retired. M. Lenepveu thought it quite correct to occupy a seat that was reserved for me, and failed to see that in so doing he was acting very improperly. He seated himself deliberately in my chair; and that caused me much sorrow.

II

Satie's connection with the 'Chat Noir' was not destined to last long. After quarrelling with the 'patron' Salis, he left abruptly and got an engagement as pianist at the Auberge du Clou, Avenue Trudaine. Here it was that in 1891 took place the historic meeting between Erik Satie and Claude Debussy—a chance meeting that was to develop into a life-long friendship. 'The moment I saw him', wrote Satie, 'I felt drawn to him and wished I might live at his side for ever. And for thirty years I was fortunate enough to see my wish fulfilled'.

A great deal has been written about the Satie-Debussy relationship, and especially in connection with the alleged 'influence' of Satie on Debussy's technique and general aesthetic. It may well be—indeed it is difficult to avoid the conviction—that

[8] Journal of the S.I.M., November 1912.

Debussy was willing to listen to Satie, and admired at least his early works—such as the *Gymnopédies* two of which he took upon himself to orchestrate so as to introduce them to the public of the Parisian Société Nationale. We know, too, that they discussed the problems of opera together at a time when Satie had already started to compose one on the *Princesse Maleine* of Maeterlinck, while Debussy, curiously enough, was toying with the idea of writing one on another Maeterlinckian text which had come his way—*Pelléas et Mélisande*. We shall probably never know exactly what occurred, but the facts are that Satie tore up his manuscript while Debussy went ahead with his. On the completion of *Pelléas* Satie, who was greatly impressed by Debussy's masterpiece, wrote to Jean Cocteau: 'Plus rien à faire de ce côté-là; il faut chercher autre chose ou je suis perdu.' What we do know however is that Debussy himself repeated to Jean Cocteau a phrase of Satie's which, he declared, 'determined the æsthetic of *Pelléas*'. And it would be difficult to be more categoric than that. The phrase in question was the following:

There is no need for the orchestra to grimace when a character comes on the stage. Do the trees in the scenery grimace? What we have to do is to create a musical scenery, a musical atmosphere in which the characters move and talk. No 'couplets'—no 'Leitmotiv', but aim at creating a certain atmosphere that suggests Puvis de Chavannes.

Now let us hear Satie on the same subject. In the course of a lecture on Debussy he said: 'Debussy's aesthetic is symbolist in some of his works and impressionist in most. Please forgive me—for am I not a little bit responsible? That's what people say. Here is the explanation. When I first met him . . . . he was full of Mussorgsky, and very conscientiously was seeking a path which he had difficulty in finding. In that respect I was much better off than he was, for my progress was not slowed down by any *Prizes*, whether from *Rome* or any other town since I don't carry that sort of thing on me or on my back, because I'm a type rather like Adam (the "Paradise" Adam) who never won a prize—a lazy type, no doubt. At that time I was writing music for *Le Fils des Étoiles* on a text by Joseph Péladan, and I explained to Debussy the necessity for a Frenchmen to free himself from the Wagnerian adventure which in no way corresponded to our national aspirations. And I told him that I was not anti-Wagner in any way but that we ought to have our own music—if possible without *choucroute*. Why shouldn't we make use of the methods employed by Claude Monet, Cézanne, Toulouse-

Suzanne Valadon. *Sketch by Erik Satie*

' The
Velvet
Gentleman '

Satie's lodging at Arcueil

Lautrec, etc . . . .? Nothing simpler. Aren't they just expressions? That would have been the origin of a new start which would have led to results which would be almost bound to be successful —and profitable too . . . . Who could have provided him with examples? Show him new discoveries? Point out to him the ground to be explored? Give him the benefit of one's experience? Who? I don't wish to answer; I am no longer interested.'

Apart from internal evidence, this is really all we have to go on with regard to the vexed question of 'influences' as between the two composers. Probably if the truth were known, each owed the other more than he cared to admit.

As to the character of their peculiar friendship, it has been described by Debussy's great friend, Louis Laloy, as 'stormy, but indissoluble'. 'They were like two brothers', said Laloy, 'the one rich, the other poor; the one generous but conscious of his superiority; the other unhappy beneath his jester's mask, hiding his feeling of inferiority, but keeping up his jokes in order to amuse his host; both on guard against one another, but all the time bound by the ties of a genuine affection'. It is clear, too, that Satie must have been on fairly intimate terms with Debussy over a considerable period. He used to go to his house regularly once a week, where the piano was put at his disposal; and he was often a guest at Debussy's table (where, however, he was only allowed as a special treat to share the finer wines, being usually provided with a carafe of 'ordinaire' for his own use). Yet Debussy clearly appreciated Satie's originality and showed his friendship and esteem in many small ways. He used to send him signed copies of his works, often with a charming dedication, such as that which accompanied, for example, the presentation copy of his Baudelaire *Poèmes*:

No. 45. Pour Erik Satie, musicien médiéval et doux, égaré dans ce siècle pour la joie de son bien amical Claude Debussy. 27 Oct. '92.

Nevertheless, it must be placed on record that towards the end of his life, when Satie began to be famous and enjoy some measure of popularity and prosperity, he suffered acutely from the silence of his old friend who seemed to have deserted him. It must not be forgotten that by that time Debussy was a sick man, with plenty of troubles of his own and living more or less the life of a recluse; and the news that reached him as he lay dying of Satie's sudden emergence into fame puzzled him and made him think he was perhaps being victimised or the object of a hoax. And until he received the bitter letter of reproaches which Satie,

33

in exasperation at what appeared to be treachery on the part of his old friend, addressed to him on his death-bed, Debussy had not perhaps realised how deeply the other had been wounded by his apparent indifference. After reading it, he crumpled up the letter and murmured, with tears in his eyes, 'Pardon'. Satie, in his turn, a few weeks before his own death, had occasion to apologise to a friend over some trivial incident, and in so doing exclaimed: 'What suffering I must have caused Debussy when he was ill' . . . . So the broken friendship was ultimately, though too late for this earth, atoned for, and one can only hope that it has been since renewed in the Elysian fields. . . . .

III

DURING THE YEARS IN which he frequented the Auberge du Clou Satie mixed with painters as well as musicians and found their company congenial. As he remarked later, he learnt more about music from painters than he ever did from musicians. It was about this time, too, that he formed a liaison with a gifted young woman who was later to become a very well-known artist herself, and the mother of another who is to-day an international celebrity.

Satie was now a full-fledged Montmartre Bohemian. He wore a beard, a top-hat and a flowing 'Lavallière', and settled down in a room on the Butte at No. 6 rue Cortot, which he furnished with benches, a table and a wooden chest. Every Sunday he would go to dine with his brother Conrad and the two would indulge in long and friendly philosophical and artistic discussions. He kept up his friendship with Contamine de Latour, and entered into collaboration with another literary friend, Albert Tinchant. Whether this 'collaboration' bore any tangible fruit is not clear, although on one occasion the newspapers announced the first performance, at the Grand Theatre at Bordeaux, of 'an opera in three Acts, poem by Albert Tinchant, music by Erik Satie, entitled *Le Bâtard de Tristan*'. ('Tristan's Bastard'!) Needless to say, this was never performed, and it is doubtful whether it ever had any existence at all outside the imagination of its authors.

In collaboration with Contamine de Latour, however, Satie did produce a three-act Ballet called *Uspud* which he submitted to the Director of the Paris Opéra. The latter did not even condescend to acknowledge the receipt of the MS, and this so infuriated the composer that he sent his seconds to the

34

unfortunate Director and challenged him to a duel! After a personal interview the affair was settled, but *Uspud* never saw the light of day, although in 1895 the two authors published a brochure[9] containing the text and some musical extracts from the Ballet, and had the temerity to announce on the cover that *Uspud* was 'presented' at the Opéra on 20th December 1892!

They also announced at the same time another ballet to be called *Ontrotance* which would be followed, 'if God were willing', by three more, rejoicing respectively in the titles of *Corcleru*, *Irnebizolle*, and *Tumisrudebude*.

A peculiarity of this 'Ballet' is that it contains only one personage—Uspud himself, accompanied by 'spiritualities'—and is dedicated to 'the Most High Luminous and Permanent Indivisibility of the Three Persons of the Holy Trinity'. A further account of this extraordinary creation will be found in Chapter VIII.

Whether this elucubration was the result of Satie's reading Flaubert's *La Tentation de Saint Antoine*, which had been one of his favourite books at the time of his military service, it is difficult to say, and the absence of any score makes it impossible to make any comment on the music. But as an indication of Satie's state of mind at that time, when his head was full of medieval legends and mystic revelations, it is clearly not without interest.

This phase in Satie's evolution, however, was relatively not of long duration, and may be said to have come to an end about the year 1895. For the next two years he seems to have produced nothing; and when he broke this silence in 1897 with the *Pièces Froides* (*Airs à faire fuir*, and *Danses de Travers*) a change of attitude and of style is discernible. No longer was he composing 'on his knees' as in previous years; henceforward he was to strike out a new line for himself in which an improved technique was allied to an extremely individual mode of utterance which seemed to open up new possibilities of musical expression. It was not the scale or dimensions of his works that were important at this stage (or indeed at any other); he remained to the last a miniaturist in music (if we except what is perhaps his masterpiece *Socrate*, written near the end of his life) but a miniaturist who somehow contrived to pack into the small forms in which he mostly worked a content so rich that it seems to overflow the narrow boundaries by which it is ostensibly confined. The virtue of this music, in fact, lies in its power to suggest to the imagina-

[9]See illustration p. 26.

35

tion more than it actually states ; its message is conveyed, as it were, by a kind of radiation, by which its meaning is extended, just as even the smallest pebble thrown into a lake may set up an infinite series of ever-widening ripples.   .

Many people are deceived by the extreme surface simplicity of Satie's music which they mistake for 'poverty'; but as Cocteau has observed[10]: 'There are certain works of art whose whole importance lies in their depth; the size of their orifice is of small account.' But in the 'eighties and early 'nineties, when Satie's 'still, small voice' first made itself heard, the public's ears were tuned to strains of a very different kind, and European music seemed definitely to be heading in a direction totally opposed to the one to which this music of Satie's seemed timidly to be pointing. In the welter of over-luscious, over-complex sonorities which the late nineteenth century so assiduously cultivated, what place could be found for anything quite so tenuous and transparent as those modest *Gymnopédies* whose limpid cadences evoke visions of barefooted dancers silhouetted on a Grecian urn? Or for the grave *Gnossiennes* with their supple rhythm and fluid modal harmonies? Yet it was in these early works that the authentic voice of Satie may be discerned most clearly; and the appearance in 1897 of the *Pièces Froides* marks a return to the earlier manner and the definite adoption of a style and æsthetic already implicit in the works written before the 'mystic' Rose + Croix period, when, as we have seen, he was exposed to certain extra-musical influences. The outward circumstances of Satie's life were also changing at this time. His Montmartre days were drawing to an end; he felt the need of a change of scenery and environment; and in 1898 he descended from the Butte, crossed Paris from north to south and took up his abode in the little suburb of Arcueil-Cachan outside the southern gates of the city, where he was to live for the remainder of his life.

Chapter III

Life at Arcueil; exploration and discoveries; The Schola Cantorum.
first public recognition; the 'humoristic' period

A FOREIGN VISITOR TO Paris, or for that matter even a Parisian, might well spend years in the capital without ever setting

[10]In *Le Coq et l'Arlequin.*

foot in the little suburb of Arcueil-Cachan, or indeed, without even knowing of its existence. To reach this rather forlorn corner of the Parisian *banlieue* one must penetrate to the southernmost confines of the city beyond the Parc de Montsouris and, crossing the Boulevard Jourdan, go out by what used to be the Porte de Gentilly. The air here is generally impregnated with the odour of the tanning factories which are congregated near by, and the landscape is one of gaunt shabby houses and dreary streets bordered by allotments and waste ground sprinkled with the ramshackle huts and rustic cabins of the local market-gardeners. Here and there a factory chimney rears its smoky head, and in front of the tall grey houses children play in the cobbled streets. What was there in this rather sordid *décor* that appealed so strongly to Satie that, while still a young man, he decided to make his home there? Did it perhaps seem to him a fitting habitation for 'Monsieur le Pauvre'? It may be; for he is reported to have said: 'Dans ce coin on y devine le séjour mystérieux de Notre-Dame Bassesse'.[11] At all events in the autumn of 1898 he transported his goods and chattels on a hand-barrow from his Montmartre lodgings, and installed himself at Arcueil in a room over a *bistrot* on the second floor of a gaunt corner house known as 'Les Quatre Cheminées', at 22 rue Cauchy. This was to be his home until he died; but no other human being except himself ever set foot during his lifetime in that mysterious room. Before settling there he had passed a night or two in the room when he came to engage it, but he was disturbed by mosquitos on that occasion which, he said, had 'certainly been sent by the Free-Masons'. He did his own cleaning, and in the evening could be seen, pitcher in hand, going to draw water from the public fountain in the square. At that time he was usually dressed from head to foot in grey velvet, a habit that earned for him among his friends at that time the nickname of the 'Velvet Gentleman'. He had bought with a small legacy no less than a dozen suits of this material, most of which were never worn and perished eventually under the onslaught of generations of clothes-moths. He also bought himself hundreds of stiff collars, of which large quantities were found in his room after his death, together with piles of shirts and waistcoats. His appearance in this dingy neighbourhood naturally excited some comment at first. But as the years wore on he was accepted by the natives as one of themselves, and in due course he began to take a prominent part in the life of the little township, joining the local

[11] 'Our Lady of Lowliness'.

Radical-Socialist Committee and eventually being decorated
with the 'Palmes Académiques' which he received from the
hands of the Prefect of the Seine representing the Government,
on July 4th, 1909. The ceremony took place at the Mairié of
Arcueil-Cachan, and was followed by a reception and informal
concert at which two of Satie's music-hall songs (*Tendrement*
and *Je te Veux* written for the Montmartre singer Paulette
Darty) were sung by local amateurs. The 'civic services' which
had earned him his decoration referred to his activities in a
charitable organisation concerned with the welfare of poor
children. Satie adored children, and took up this voluntary work
as it gave him opportunities of taking charge of parties of children on outings and sight-seeing expeditions. On one occasion,
hearing that a strictly limited number of school-children were
going on some excursion he got up a subscription among his
friends and neighbours, and wrote to the Mayor asking for permission to bring another dozen children himself for whom he
would be personally responsible.

Among his other local activities must be counted the organisation of concerts and *fêtes*; the foundation of a 'Regional
Group', comprising Normandy, Maine, Anjou and Poitou; and
journalistic work on the local newspaper where he was responsible for a regular feature which gave him a magnificent opportunity of indulging his peculiar vein of drollery in print. He was
not slow to take advantage of this, as the following examples of
his somewhat unconventional contributions will attest: (I quote
from M. Templier's monograph)

BITTEN BY A MONKEY—
is not so agreeable as a visit to
60 rue Emile-Raspail—chez l'Ami
Jacob—where the dancing classes
'La Marguerite' are held.

NO MORE BALD HEADS—
if everyone took care to belong to
the new Savings Society 'The Aqueduct'.
Spend what you save on a hair-lotion.

But his activities at Arcueil were only a small part of his life;
indeed he still spent most of his days (and often nights) in Montmartre where for a time he was associated with the famous
'chansonnier' Vincent Hyspa whose accompaniments he used to
play at *soirées* in private houses. These were years of poverty for
Satie and he was obliged to earn his living as best he could.
Hence the 'pot-boilers' he wrote for the music-hall singer

Paulette Darty. But even when he was experimenting in this way in the idiom of the *café-concert* Satie refused to allow his art to be corrupted. He called what he wrote under these conditions 'rudes saloperies', but he probably derived a certain satisfaction from being able to write in this vein on a level where nothing is required of music except that it shall give pleasure. And he was obviously not insensitive to the 'poetry' of the music-hall, which later was to become part of the aesthetic creed of those young musicians who were to acclaim Satie as their guide, philosopher and friend. He sensed obscurely in those Montmartre days the truth of those aphorisms that Cocteau was to enunciate many years afterwards—such as that 'The music-hall, the circus and American negro bands fertilise an artist just as life does', or 'The Café-Concert is often pure; the theatre is always corrupt'. And so, round about 1900, Satie was writing not only the sentimental *Valses Chantées—Je te Veux* and *Poudre d'Or*, but also that remarkable *La Diva de l'Empire* which, with its sideways glance across the Channel to Leicester Square, may be considered as a sort of synthesis, a stylization of the Anglo-American 'Rag-time' idiom which was to be exploited later, in the years following the first German war, but with more sophistication and conscious *parti pris*, by some of his young disciples. And Satie himself in later years was to make further allusions to those Transatlantic rhythms—in the Ballet *Parade*. But the interesting thing about these early 'Montmartre' compositions is that they show that Satie, even when aping the methods and language of the circus and music-hall, somehow managed to preserve all his innate candour and purity of style—the same purity that can be perceived in such works as the *Gymnopédies* or the *Gnossiennes*.

Another work that dates from this period—it was composed in 1899—is the delightful *Jack-in-the-Box* written for a pantomime which was never produced. The manuscript was found among his papers after Satie's death and published posthumously in a skilful and sympathetic orchestral version made by Darius Milhaud for the Russian Ballet who included it in their repertoire in 1926.

The three *Morceaux en forme de Poire* for piano duet were composed four years later, and show Satie at his best. They were written in answer to some advice alleged to have been given him by Debussy to the effect that he should pay more attention to form; they are also a mild satire on the theories held by the Impressionist school in general. As Cocteau puts it: 'The Impressionist composers cut a pear into twelve pieces and gave

39

each piece the title of a poem. Then Satie composed twelve poems and entitled the whole *Morceaux en forme de Poire.*' At all events they mark the beginning of a new phase in Satie's evolution and were his last important work before he took the step which was to influence profoundly the remainder of his career.

In 1905, in his fortieth year, he decided to go to school again to perfect his technique and acquire a thorough grounding in counterpoint and theory which had always eluded him during his student days at the Conservatoire. And so he decided to enter that austere institution, the Schola Cantorum, presided over at that time by the august Vincent d'Indy, the distinguished disciple of Franck and upholder of the Franckist tradition. For a man of his age it was a remarkable decision and must have called for a considerable degree of moral courage. There was also a certain risk attaching to such a step, for as Debussy warned him: 'A votre âge on ne change plus de peau'. To which however Satie bravely retorted that if he failed it would only mean that he hadn't got it in him to be a composer.

The whole episode demolishes, I think completely, the accusations and charges commonly brought against him by the anti-Satieists who pretend that he was never anything but a *farceur*, a leg-puller, a bungling amateur, who tried to conceal his mediocrity behind a façade of pretentious nonsense. On the contrary, both his actions and his words, as on this occasion, prove conclusively, if additional proof were needed, the essential integrity and artistic humility of Satie whose whole life conformed to the precept which he himself laid down—namely that 'Those who practise an art must live in a state of complete renunciation'.

His work may be open to criticism on purely aesthetic grounds, like that of any other composer, but any attempt to impugn his artistic integrity or suggest that he was ever insincere, is quite simply inadmissible. The evidence is too strongly weighted in a contrary sense. Probably no other musician was ever so reviled and mocked at by his contemporaries as Satie; but the hostility he aroused never caused him to swerve an inch from the path he had set himself to tread; and whatever his limitations may have been, all those who knew him really well will agree that he possessed what must always be an artist's strongest asset—the integrity of a saint and a determination to defend to the last whatever he felt to be true. He was, in fact, almost equally indifferent to praise or insults; 'to seek intentionally to give pleasure or the reverse', as Cocteau observes, 'seemed to him an incomprehensible attitude. Without hesitation he would take up an untenable position'. And only a few days before his death did he not reassert to one of his disciples the principle which had guided him throughout his life—'Il faut être intransigeant jusqu'au bout'? Naïve, perhaps, but surely an attitude worthy of respect? And, quite apart from any other considerations, had he been what his detractors in their ignorance would like to have us believe, it is, to say the least, unlikely that he would have gained the respect and esteem of men like Debussy, Ravel, Stravinsky, Picasso, Braque, Koechlin, Cocteau, d'Indy, Roussel, Milhaud, Honegger, Poulenc, Auric and many other distinguished artists. No; whatever his adversaries may proclaim to the contrary, Erik Satie must be recognised as a serious artist; only on that basis can any criticism be valid. Once that point is conceded, however, the discussion is open, and any opinion may be legitimately held with regard to the intrinsic merits or short-comings of his works.

At the Schola, at all events, he was regarded as an excellent pupil, and at the end of three years, in June 1908, he obtained his Diploma in Counterpoint, signed by d'Indy and Roussel with the mention 'Très Bien'. We know moreover that Roussel in particular had a high opinion of Satie and said of him that he was 'prodigieusement musicien'—high praise indeed coming from such a quarter.

However Satie's decision to put himself under the tutelage of d'Indy and the music he composed while under the influence of the teaching of the Schola brought down upon him criticism as violent as that which his earlier works had provoked. Only whereas before he had been criticised for being too simple and untutored, now he was blamed for being too academic. Satie expressed his bewilderment in a letter to his brother when Ravel and other musicians who were interested in him were preparing to introduce some of his early works to the public through the medium of the Société Musicale Indépendante (S.M.I.). This was in 1910. 'In 1905', he wrote, 'I began to study with d'Indy. I was tired of being reproached for my ignorance—an ignorance of which I was fully aware since competent judges had detected signs of it in my works. After three years' hard work I obtained at the Schola Cantorum my Diploma in Counterpoint signed by the hand of my most excellent master and the best and most learned man who ever walked this earth. So there I was, in 1908 in possession of a licence conferring on me the title of Contrapuntist. Proud of my learning I set to work to compose. My first work of this kind was a Chorale and Fugue for Piano duet (*Aperçus désagréables*).[12] I have often been insulted in the course of my miserable existence, but never before was I treated with such contempt. "What on earth had I been doing with d'Indy? The things I had written before were so full of charm—And now? merely pretentious and boring". Whereupon the "young ones" start a campaign against d'Indy, and begin playing things like the *Sarabandes*, and the *Fils des Etoiles*, etc., works which were once considered to be evidence of my appalling ignorance—quite wrongly, as these young men now assert. And that, my dear fellow, is how life is; one can't make head or tail of it. . . . .'

Nevertheless Ravel and his friends arranged a Satie programme at one of the S.M.I. concerts on January 16, 1911, Ravel himself playing the second *Sarabande*, the Prelude to the *Fils des Etoiles* and the third *Gymnopédie*. A programme note paid the following tribute to the composer who was now for the first time to be acclaimed by the élite of the Parisian musical world:

Erik Satie occupies a very special place in the history of contemporary art. Isolated and aloof from the times in which he lives he has already written some short pieces which prove him to be a 'forerunner' of genius. These works, unhappily too few in number, are surprising for the way in which they anticipated the modernist vocabulary, and for the almost prophetic character of certain harmonic inventions which they contain. . . . M. Claude Debussy paid a striking tribute to this subtle 'explorer' by orchestrating two of his *Gymnopédies* which were performed at a concert of the Société Nationale; while M. Maurice Ravel, by playing today the second *Sarabande*, which bears the astounding date of 1887, bears witness to the esteem which is felt by the most 'advanced' composers for the creator who a quarter of a century ago was already speaking the daring musical 'jargon' of tomorrow.[13]

The public was delighted with these examples of Satie's genius, and the critics of the progressive school took Satie to their hearts. Calvocoressi and others wrote enthusiastic articles and Satie thoroughly enjoyed his triumph. The only fly in the ointment was the absence of his old friend Debussy who was then on bad terms with Ravel and annoyed that the latter should have been responsible for presenting his protégé's work to the public. And yet, a few months later, when he himself conducted

[12]Satie at one time thought of turning this into a String Quartet.
[13]Quoted by P. Templier.

42

his own arrangement of the *Gymnopédies* at the Cercle Musical, he was surprised at the warmth of their reception. Satie was pained. 'Why won't he allow me just a little corner in his shade? .... I don't want to take any of his sun.'

Nevertheless, for the first time in his career he was beginning to be something like a celebrity. Following Debussy's example, another of his admirers, the young Roland-Manuel, made an orchestral arrangement of the Prelude to the *Porte Héroïque du Ciel* and conducted it at a concert of the S.M.I. The work was very well received and Satie's supporters, (the 'Satieists') began an active propaganda on his behalf, proposing him as a candidate for the title of 'Prince of Musicians'. Satie's own comment on this manœuvre was characteristic: 'The Prince of Musicians will not be rich, poor fellow'.[14] In any case all this gave him fresh courage, and he set to work with renewed ardour. Now his works are sought after by the publishers; Rouart-Lerolle bring out his early piano pieces and ask for more. So does the firm of Demets, for whom he writes the *Véritables Préludes Flasques* which inaugurate the new 'linear' style which characterises most of the music of the post-Schola period. Another work which exhibits these tendencies is the Suite for orchestra, better known in the version for piano duet, consisting of two Chorales and two Fugues to which he gave the enigmatic title of *En Habit de Cheval* (1911). The allusion here, is not, the composer explained, to the dress of the rider, but to that of the horse—'for example, two shafts attached to a four-wheel cart'. Some critics have seen in this a reference to the rules and regulations formulated by the theorists which hamper the progress of the 'free' musician; and it is quite possible he had something of the kind in mind.

Ever since the piano pieces of 1890 Satie had formed the habit of inserting mysterious directions to the player over the music, which was usually written at that time without either bar-lines or time or key signatures. Thus in the first *Gnossienne* (1890) one finds such indications as 'Très luisant', 'Du bout de la pensée', 'Sur la langue'; while in the *Danse de travers* (1897) one passage is marked 'être visible un moment', another 'un peu

[14]But he evidently took the suggestion very seriously and was indignant at the opposition it aroused in certain quarters. Thus on July 3rd, 1912, he wrote to Roland-Manuel: '. . . It's quite disgusting, my dear fellow. These dolts are completely ignorant. Ecorcheville, who is guided by Vuillermoz refuses to pay any attention to what you told him about the P. of M. But don't let's give up, in Heaven's name; we can't do that. PS. Don't let's get upset about it; we must go into the question calmly; music needs a Prince and she shall have one, by God. Your old pal, E. S.'

cuit', another 'en y regardant à deux fois', and so on. In the
works of his 'mystic' period the indications were sometimes
unusual, (e.g., 'très sincèrement silencieux', 'avec un grand
oubli du présent') but not humoristic, and generally intelligible
as having some relation to the music. But as the composer grew
older, and especially during the years following his Schola Cantorum experience when he was beginning to be a celebrity, i.e.,
from 1908 to 1916, his fantasy became more and more exuberant.
To the pieces he now began to issue he gave more and more
grotesque titles and a regular 'running commentary' of quips
and nonsensical remarks was often superimposed upon the
music. The latter frequently contains parodies of or allusions to
popular and classical music—a well-known example is the introduction into one of the *Embryons Desséchés* of a few bars of
Chopin's Funeral March which is described as a well-known
Mazurka by Schubert . . . But almost invariably the nonsense
is brilliantly executed from a purely musical point of view, and
all these pieces, if divested of their literary or humoristic content,
can quite well stand on their own legs and be judged on their
merits purely as music.

This brings us to the question of what importance we may
suppose the composer to have attached to these wise-cracks and
to the comic titles it amused him to give to his music.

We may believe, with Cocteau, that he adopted these peculiar
methods mainly as a mask and 'in order to protect his works
from persons obsessed by the sublime', or, with Cortot, that the
verbal commentary is an integral part of his musical conception.
According to the first theory Satie undoubtedly felt he had something new to say, but he was perhaps secretly a little unsure of
himself and doubtful about securing for his rather unassuming
music the recognition to which he felt it was entitled. He therefore hit upon the idea of giving his compositions grotesque titles
and furnishing them with a humorous text so as to disarm the
critics in advance. If they were discerning enough they would be
able to appreciate the real value of the music underneath its
fantastic presentation; if not, then it would be easy for them to
dismiss it all as a joke. And that suited Satie's book very well.
For though he was immensely in earnest about his music he
loved mystification, and nothing gave him greater pleasure than
upsetting the pundits and putting them off the scent. In addition
there was, of course, a deliberate desire to parody the somewhat
'precious' titles favoured by Debussy and the Impressionists—
e.g., *Et la lune descend sur le temple qui fut*, *La terrasse des audiences*

au clair de lune; while, if a precedent were needed, he could always claim to be merely following the example of the 18th century clavecinists and notably Couperin the Great who was very fond of such titles as *Le tic-toc-choc ou les Maillotins, Les Coucous bénévoles, Les Barricades mystérieuses,* or *Les vieux galants et les Trésorières surannées.* (Cf. Satie's *Trois Valses du Précieux Dégôuté* or his *Vieux Séquins et vieilles cuirasses.*)[15]

Alfred Cortot, on the other hand,[16] maintains that the prose commentaries which accompany all the piano pieces of this period (1897-1915) are an essential part of Satie's intentions and not merely added to put the critics off the scent. In many cases, it is true, the text does seem to have a direct bearing on the music, but not by any means always. For example, the *Sonatine Bureaucratique* is a perfectly straightforward piece of abstract music and could quite well dispense with the absurd narration which has been superimposed.

On the other hand, in *Sports et Divertissements* (1914) the text is almost as important as the music. These delightful little thumbnail sketches, twenty in number, were composed to a definite 'programme', and were intended as a musical counterpart to a set of drawings by the artist Charles Martin illustrating such subjects as Fishing, Yachting, Flirting, Golf, The Swing, Tennis, etc. To each of these Satie added a verbal description in his own inimitable style which is really inseparable from the music.

Incidentally these little pieces, which we shall be examining in more detail in another chapter, are among Satie's happiest efforts; indeed, Darius Milhaud went so far as to assert that they are outstanding in French music. And from a literary point of view the commentaries are certainly as amusing and neatly turned as anything he ever perpetrated in the way of textual embellishments to his music.

And yet Satie was absolutely opposed to any reading aloud of his verbal texts during performance, and specifically stated his objection to this in a 'Warning' which serves as a Preface to his *Heures séculaires et instantanées* written in June and July, 1914. This pronouncement has the same didactic and aggressive tone as some of his earlier manifestos issued when he was still

[15]The same thing had also been done, but less elaborately by Rossini in his *Péchés de ma Vieillesse* which included such titles as 'Butter Variations', 'Hygienic Prelude for Morning Use', and 'Miscarriage of a Polka-Mazurka'. These tunes, if not the titles, are familiar to all balletomanes as they are used in *La Boutique Fantasque.*

[16]See 'Le Cas Erik Satie' *Revue Musicale,* avril-mai, 1938.

45

The Life

imbued with the mystico-religious ideas it pleased him to profess when posing as a 'Seer'. It is addressed to an imaginary 'Whosoever' who might be tempted to take liberties with his creations, and runs as follows:

I forbid the text to be read out loud during the performance of the music. Failure to conform with these instructions will cause the transgressor to incur my just indignation.

Cortot points out that this 'warning' implies that Satie himself did attach some importance to the literary side of this particular work, at any rate, which is a kind of monologue accompanied by music of a definitely descriptive nature. But there are also plenty of examples of pieces where the 'literary' comment'seems completely irrelevant, adding nothing to the music which could well be divorced from the accompanying text without being affected in any way. There is something else, too, that has an important bearing on the whole of this aspect of the 'Satie problem,' and that is the fact that he was, after all, a wit as well as a musician and liked to express himself in writing. And some o his purely literary productions are distinguished by a certain verbal facility, a felicity of phrase, and a kind of crazy logic that would not disgrace a Lewis Carroll or a Sidney Smith. One of the best examples of Satie's peculiar and very individual *esprit* is to be found in his *Mémoires d'un amnésique* ('Memoirs of a sufferer from amnesia'—the title alone is deliciously *bien trouvé*) which was published in the journal of the Société Internationale de Musique in 1913. It is here that can be found the famous 'Day in the life of a Musician' which is worth quoting in full. The French text is given as Appendix C.1.

An artist must regulate his life.

Here is a time-table of my daily acts. I rise at 7.18; am inspired from 10.23 to 11.47. I lunch at 12.11 and leave the table at 12.14. A healthy ride on horse-back round my domain follows from 1.19 p.m. to 2.53 p.m. Another bout of inspiration from 3.12 to 4.7 p.m. From 5 to 6.47 p.m. various occupations (fencing, reflection, immobility, visits, contemplation, dexterity, natation, etc.)

Dinner is served at 7.16 and finished at 7.20 p.m. From 8.9 to 9.59 p.m. symphonic readings (out loud). I go to bed regularly at 10.37 p.m. Once a week (on Tuesdays) I awake with a start at 3.14 a.m.

My only nourishment consists of food that is white: eggs, sugar, shredded bones, the fat of dead animals, veal, salt, coco-nuts, chicken cooked in white water, mouldy fruit, rice, turnips, sausages in camphor, pastry, cheese (white varieties), cotton salad, and certain kinds of fish (without their skin). I boil my wine and drink it cold

mixed with the juice of the Fuchsia. I have a good appetite, but never talk when eating for fear of strangling myself.
I breathe carefully (a little at a time) and dance very rarely. When walking I hold my ribs and look steadily behind me.
My expression is very serious; when I laugh it is unintentional, and I always apologise very politely.
I sleep with only one eye closed, very profoundly. My bed is round with a hole in it for my head to go through. Every hour a servant takes my temperature and gives me another.

This might almost be a page from the Nonsense Book by Edward Lear; but sometimes Satie's humour takes on a more Lewis Carrollian twist, as in this quip with its falsely logical air: 'Although our information is inaccurate we do not guarantee it'.

The same spirit of impish nonsensicality can be observed in another work written about this time (it is dated 1913 but was not produced until after the war in 1921)—*Le Piège de Méduse* described as: 'Comédie en un acte de M. Erik Satie(avec musique du même monsieur)'. The interesting thing about this work (one of Satie's first incursions into the theatre, if we except the charming little *Geneviève de Brabant* composed in 1899 for a marionette theatre, and fragments of an operetta *Pousse-l'Amour* dating from 1905) is that it might so easily and appropriately be described as 'Dada' except that the 'Dadaist' movement in the arts had not yet been invented (see Chapter V). It thus affords yet another illustration of Satie's extraordinary faculty of anticipating and creating the prototype of almost every genre that years later was to become fashionable and elevated into an aesthetic cult. The dancing monkey Jonas, 'stuffed by a master hand', the Baron Méduse and his 'foster-daughter' ('fille de lait'!) Frisette and manservant Polycarpe, and the absurd situations in which they find themselves, are pure 'Dada' and belong far more to the year 1921 when Pierre Bertin produced the piece than to 1913—when it was written.

I shall be returning in a later chapter to the subject of Satie's literary excursions; in the meantime we have seen how most of the music written between 1897 and 1916 was made to run, as it were, in double harness with this spirit of freakishness which the composer seems to have inherited from his uncle 'Sea-Bird' and which was, it must be recognised, a fundamental part of his nature. We have seen, too, how the peculiar methods he adopted in presenting his music to the public—the method, as one critic has called it, of 'protective irony'—succeeded only too well in diverting the attention of some listeners (especially Anglo-Saxon

47

ones) from the substance to the shadow. For, failing to see any sublimity in Satie's music, they only see in it what was meant to be ridiculous. The comic disguise does its work too well: the mask is mistaken for the man.

But the period we have been reviewing was not the only one, or even the most significant, in the composer's evolution; and it was during the World War of 1914-1918 that he was to enter upon a new phase in his career, the one in which he may be truly said to have 'found himself'.

Chapter IV

The War years and fame; collaboration with Cocteau and Diaghilev; Parade; *'Les Six'; death of Debussy;* Socrate

WHEN WORLD WAR I broke out Satie, as we have seen, was beginning to be something of a celebrity in Parisian musical circles. His works had been published and played in public by pianists of the first rank, such as Ricardo Viñes; Ravel and Debussy both took an interest in him and had conducted or played his music; and the critics had written flattering articles about him. In the meantime the 'Prince of Musicians', always carrying his legendary umbrella, his shrewd eyes glinting through his pince-nez, and his quizzical, be-whiskered face crowned invariably by a bowler hat, was becoming a familiar sight as he trudged through the streets of Paris, engaged on who knows what mysterious errands . . . For he always went everywhere on foot—an idiosyncracy which drew from Cocteau this touching tribute: 'Another poet whom the angels guide, cherish and torment is Erik Satie, who walks every night from Montmartre or Montparnasse to his home at Arcueil-Cachan—a miracle which cannot be explained unless the angels carry him . . .'

He was forty-eight when France was called upon to defend her frontiers against the German onslaught in August 1914, and the rhythm of his life was interrupted by the war in common with all his fellow-citizens, although he affected a certain indifference to the events which were shaking the world. Nevertheless he had military duties to perform, and was envied for this by his old friend Debussy who was four years his senior and already suffering from the disease that was to kill him before the war was over. Debussy was completely bowled over by the catastrophe, and tormented by a consciousness of his own uselessness and inability to take an active part in the struggle. 'What I am doing', he wrote to his publisher Durand in August 1914, 'seems so wretchedly small and unimportant. I can even envy Satie who, as a Corporal, is preparing seriously to defend Paris'.

How seriously we do not know; but it is probable that Satie derived a certain amount of amusement from seeing himself in a new role as a defender of Paris; although it would seem as if his duties were confined to patrolling the streets of Arcueil-Cachan. Later on, when the air-raids on Paris began, we are told that he would seek shelter with his neighbours, announcing his arrival with the words: 'I'm coming to die with you', uttered in a sepulchral low voice . . .[17]

But in spite of all the dangers and discomforts of these dreadful days, the war years were to give Satie one of the biggest chances of his life and bring him into contact with artists of world-wide renown. It began when in 1915 he made the acquaintance in Paris of Jean Cocteau, poet, dramatist, brilliant *animateur*, and leader of the literary advance guard.

Cocteau was then preparing an adaptation of *A Midsummer Night's Dream*, and invited Satie to write incidental music for this production. His contribution took the form of *Cinq Grimaces*, but the project was never realised and the music never performed. But next year, after hearing and being greatly impressed by the *Morceaux en forme de Poire*, Cocteau invited Satie to collaborate with him and Picasso in a ballet he had been commissioned to write for Serge de Diaghilev, whose Russian company had swept triumphantly through Europe in the years immediately preceding the war. Diaghilev was then in Rome, with his troupe, and it was there that work was begun in the spring of 1915 on the ballet *Parade* which was to burst like a bomb in Paris two years later when it was produced at the Châtelet in one of the most critical years of the war. It was revolutionary to a degree which had no parallel in the history of the stage, and the public, the critics and all the *bien-pensants* musicians were duly shocked at this first manifestation of 'Cubism' in music and choreography. While Cocteau, author of the scenario, Picasso, designer of the sets and costumes, and

[17]He seems indeed to have had at least one narrow escape of which he gives an amusing account in a letter to Roland-Manuel dated March 14th, 1918: 'Old chap, it was very nearly all up with Satie the other day; I was damn nearly killed; terribly near me the bombs were. Was I scared! There were some killed, but not me . . . as luck would have it. Although only a civilian I stuck it out. Such is life . . .'

Massine the choreographer were in Rome working on the early
stages of the ballet under the supervision of Diaghilev, their
musical collaborator, Erik Satie, was quietly putting together
his remarkable score in Paris—a score which, in Cocteau's
words, 'was meant to supply a musical background to suggestive
noises such as sirens, typewriters, aeroplanes and dynamos . . .'
Nearly all these noises, however (which Cocteau called 'trompe-
l'oreille' on the analogy of the 'trompe-l'oeil' employed by
painters—e.g., newspapers, imitation wood-work, etc.) had to
be omitted in performance owing to material difficulties; and
even the typewriters could hardly be heard. Nevertheless the
critics persisted in describing Satie's score as a mere din, and the
impressionist musicians, Cocteau records, 'thought the orchestra
in *Parade* poor because it had no sauce'. What the composer
had to do was to write music to a scenario representing a booth
at a fair in which the principal characters were a Chinese juggler,
a couple of acrobats, an American girl, (a parody of the type
then popular in Transatlantic films) and three showmen or
'Managers'. The action takes place outside the showmen's tent
while the actors are going through their antics to invite the
public to come inside and see the real show. Hence the title
Parade—recalling the picture of the same name by Seurat
depicting a similar scene outside a side-show at a fair.

R. H. Wilenski[18] describes *Parade* as an attempt by Picasso
and Cocteau 'to bring Flat-pattern Cubism, as it were, to life,
the subject representing the modern artists' cult of the circus,
which had continued since the 'seventies'. A real innovation was
Picasso's treatment of the Managers who were encased in
wooden frames so as to become, as Cocteau describes[19] them, 'a
kind of human scenery, animated pictures by Picasso. . . . The
problem was to take a series of natural gestures and to metamorphose them into a dance without depriving them of their
realistic force, as a modern painter seeks his inspiration in natural
objects in order to metamorphose them into pure painting, but
without losing sight of the force of their volume, substance,
colour and shade. For reality alone, even when well concealed,
has power to arouse emotion'. Commenting on this, the same
critic observes: 'The concept of the Managers was thus in line
with Picasso's Cubism where all the forms (even those which in
the final picture evoke no definable associated ideas) owe something of their vitality to the particular "real" forms from which

[18]See *Modern French Painters*, p. 257.
[19]In *Le Coq et l'Arlequin*.

they were evolved'. It is worth noting in this connection that *Parade* is described on the title-page as a 'Ballet réaliste'.

The new aesthetic implied in this unusual conception of ballet was immediately perceived and assimilated by Satie, and so, in Cocteau's words, 'gradually there came to birth a score in which Satie seems to have discovered an unknown dimension, thanks to which one can listen simultaneously both to the "parade" and to the show going on inside. . .'

The music is, in fact, fundamentally, almost disconcertingly simple, but at the same time extraordinarily suggestive and admirably adapted to the subject-matter. This is how Georges Auric describes Satie's contribution to this realist ballet in his Preface to *Parade:*

Like that of Picasso, his art does not attempt to seduce us by means of a brilliant and lively evocation. As if seeing him for the first time he shows us the quintessence of the individual human being and portrays with great clarity the most amazing characters who remind us of Rimbaud and permit us to envisage a future exempt from boredom. The terrible mysteries of China, the little American girl's night-club melancholy, the astonishing gymnastic feats of the acrobats—all the sadness of the circus is here—the nostalgia of the hurdy-gurdy which will never play Bach fugues. Satie's score is planned so as to serve as a musical background to the scenic noises and percussion which occupy the foreground. In this way it is made very humbly subservient to that 'reality' which stifles the nightingale's song beneath the noise of tramcars.

A few knowing writers, who prefer audacities which have already been tried out and the sort of fantasy which amused us the day before yesterday, drew attention to the inexperience of a musician whose lack of originality and failure to please they felt it their duty to point out. Notwithstanding, Art continues to go forward and no one can prevent her.

Commenting on the remark about the nightingales and the tramcars Constant Lambert[20] objects to the implication that Satie's music shows any specifically 'anti-Romantic' tendency, and points out that 'Satie was too objective in his standpoint to side with either the nightingales or the tramcars. If while riding on a tramcar a nightingale had flown on to the same seat he would not have seen in it a symbolisation of two opposed worlds and indulged in either philosophy or regrets. He would have accepted it quite naturally as a simple occurrence . . . There is no Romance about his music, not even of the modern type that takes the form of anti-Romanticism'. And he goes on to point

[20]See *Music Ho!* p. 90.

out that 'the most striking feature of *Parade* is its combination of monotonously repeated and mechanical figures with passages of great lyrical charm'. Both these aspects of music, in fact, the mechanical and the emotional, were equally valid for Satie; and it is this detached attitude of his towards an art which most musicians have sought to make the vehicle of transcendent and mainly subjective feelings and emotions that makes his music appear so strangely 'bare' and, in a sense, inhuman.

In the present instance he was well served by his scenario, and the music that accompanies the principal figures as they perform their 'stunts' outside the showmen's booth, culminating in the frantic but vain endeavours of the 'Managers' to persuade the public not to mistake the 'parade' for the spectacle to be seen inside the theatre, has a kind of hallucinatory quality that is quite unique. Nevertheless the Ballet was too 'advanced' for the Parisian war-time public (it was produced by the Russian Ballet at a gala performance for a war charity at the Châtelet Theatre on May 18, 1917) and had a very hostile reception. Satie, Cocteau and Picasso were stigmatised as 'Boches' in the Parisian press, and one critic so incensed Satie by his review that the composer retaliated by sending him insulting post-cards with the result that he had to appear before the magistrates and was condemned to eight days imprisonment. He did not have to go to gaol, however, as his sentence was suspended.

Nevertheless Satie was delighted at being involved with his distinguished collaborators in an artistic 'scandal' of this magnitude; it flattered him to think that he was the centre of a controversy that divided the artistic world of Paris into two camps. The only fly in his ointment was the silence of Debussy from whom, with every additional increase in his fame, Satie felt himself becoming more and more estranged. The story of their final rupture has already been related; but if Satie at this stage in his career was to lose an old friend and supporter he soon found himself at the head of a new 'movement' in which he was to play the role of Mentor to a group of young musicians who sensed in the composer of *Parade* a new force in music and the incarnation, so it seemed to them, of *'l'esprit nouveau'*—that spirit of rejuvenation of which their art was so badly in need. The young musicians who rallied round Satie at this time were later to become famous as 'Les Six'; but before they were thus designated by the critic Henri Collet (on the analogy of the Russian 'Five'—the 'Mighty Handful') Satie had dubbed them 'Les Nouveaux Jeunes'. Moreover to begin with there were only four members of the group—Georges Auric, Louis Durey, Arthur Honegger and Germaine Tailleferre; Darius Milhaud and Francis Poulenc completed the little band the following year. Satie organised a series of concerts at the Vieux Colombier at which the works of these young people were produced, and very soon they were joined by Jean Cocteau who gave them his backing and provided them with their theoretic 'Bible' in the form of a brilliant little pamphlet of aphorisms epitomising the new tendencies which they represented, and elevating Erik Satie to the position of High Priest in the new aesthetic cult. The pamphlet was called *Le Coq et l'Arlequin* (Cock and Harlequin[21]) and was dedicated by the author to Georges Auric '. . . because a musician of young age proclaims the richness and grace of a generation which no longer grimaces, or wears a mask, or hides, or shirks, and is not afraid to admire or to stand up for what it admires. It hates paradox and eclecticism. It despises their smile and faded elegance. It also shuns the colossal. That is what I call "escaping from Germany". Long live the Cock! Down with Harlequin! (N.B. Harlequin also means: "A dish composed of various scraps"—*Larousse*)'.

The pamphlet, Cocteau further explained, 'is not concerned with any existing school, but with a school to whose existence nothing points, were it not for the first-fruits of a few young artists, the efforts of the painters, and the tiredness of our ears'. A postscript contains the following words: 'I add here the *Socrate* of Satie, which was unknown to me at the moment of writing these lines'.

All this meant the final consecration of Satie as a 'chef d'école'—although he himself deprecated any suggestion that he should be considered as such, and said so specifically in one of the broad-sheets issued in 1920 by Cocteau under the title *Le Coq*. These broad-sheets, of which not more than about half a dozen were published, on coloured poster-paper with eccentric typography and facsimile reproductions of wisecracks scribbled by Satie and the 'Six', served as publicity for the Group, and have a certain documentary interest. It was on one of them that Satie made his celebrated but rather malicious jibe at the expense of his former benefactor Ravel: 'Ravel refuse la Légion d'Honneur mais toute sa musique l'accepte'. (At that time Ravel was out of favour with the 'Six' who blamed him for what they called his 'écriture artiste' and excessive 'refinement'.) In

[21]English translation by R. H. Myers, The Egoist Press, 1921; also incorporated in *A Call to Order*, Faber 1926.

another issue of *Le Coq* Satie divides musicians into two classes—
'les pions et les poètes' ('pundits and poets'). 'The former', he
declared, 'deceive both the public and the critics. Among the
poets I would place Liszt, Chopin, Schubert, Mussorgsky; among
the pundits—Rimsky-Korsakov. Debussy was the pure type of
poet-musician. Among his followers you will find several examples of pundits. (D'Indy, although he is a Professor, is not one
of these.) Mozart's technique (métier) is light, Beethoven's
heavy. This is not generally understood; but both of them are
poets; that is the important thing. *P.S.* Wagner is a dramatic
poet'.

He did not admire the Impressionists' methods of orchestration, and said so in these terms: 'With the exception of Claude
Debussy's, the cloudy (poussiéreux) orchestra of the Impressionists isn't a real orchestra at all. It's a piano orchestrated.'
For Debussy he always made an exception; and seeing how
greatly he had been harmed by a host of imitators he was
determined to prevent the same thing happening to himself.
Hence: 'I never criticise Debussy. It's only the "Debussystes"
who annoy me. There is no School of Satie. There could never
be a "Satisme"; I should be opposed to it. In art there must be
no form of slavery. I have always tried to throw off my followers
and keep them guessing both as regards the form and content of
every new work of mine. This is the only way for an artist to
avoid becoming a "chef d'école"—that is to say a pundit
(pion).'

And indeed, all his life, from the time when he was still a
student at the Conservatoire and being taken by his stepmother
to hear concerts by Guilmant and his like, Satie had had a horror of the academic 'pompier' style, and all his life he had
preserved 'a freshness of outlook and an instinctive sympathy for
new, untried paths in art which prevented him from ever stand-
ing still or repeating himself. Like Picasso, like Stravinsky, he
was continually renewing himself and seeking new methods of
expression; and now, instead of trying to repeat the kind of
success he had achieved with *Parade*, Satie was planning a work
which would be entirely unlike anything he had done hitherto.
It was indeed a surprise to all who knew the composer and his
work when they learned that he was planning to set to music
extracts from Victor Cousin's translation of the Dialogues of
Plato, centring round the figure of Socrates. His opportunity
came when he was commissioned by the Princess de Polignac
(née Singer) to write a work for her, as many composers who

54

were then celebrated and 'fashionable' had already been invited to do. The invitation came at the suggestion of Jane Bathori the singer, for whom Satie had composed his three songs *Daphénéo*, *La Statue de Bronze*, and *Le Chapelier* two years earlier. Madame Bathori had always been active in encouraging 'new' composers and making their works known, and it was she who was associated with Satie at the time when he was sponsoring the concerts at the Vieux Colombier which were the means of introducing to the public the first youthful compositions of 'Les Nouveaux Jeunes' (afterwards known as 'Les Six'). Madame de Polignac, a wealthy American-born patroness of the arts, presided over a musical 'salon' which was nothing if not up-to-date; and some of the most famous composers of the day, including Stravinsky, had dedicated specially commissioned works to her. Now it was Satie's turn to be thus honoured, and the result was *Socrate*—a 'drame symphonique' in three parts, scored for four sopranos, flute, oboe, cor anglais, clarinet, bassoon, horn, trumpet, harp, kettle-drums and strings. In this noble, if austere work which I think we must consider Satie's masterpiece, the composer seems at last to have found himself completely, and to have produced music rich in poetic content. The simple and limpid style of this deeply reflective work which flows quietly and inevitably along in an uneventful stream, flecked here and there by little eddies and whirls of subdued emotion, betokens a final mastery and controlled equilibrium to which all Satie's previous works seem to have aspired with varying degrees of success. *Socrate* is the apotheosis of that 'linear' conception of music which Satie, except during his Rose+Croix period, had deliberately cultivated, and in so doing had prepared the way for the neo-classic movement which was fashionable in the years following his death (which occurred in 1925). The ideal of the neo-classicists was, in fact, a return to that 'simplicity', that *dépouillement* or stripping of non-essentials, which had characterised so much of Satie's music and which was first manifested in the *Gymnopédies* of 1886. Scoffed at at first, and stigmatised as jejune and barren by those whose ears were intoxicated with the over-luscious harmonies and sophisticated refinements of nineteenth-century music, the Satiean aesthetic gradually won acceptance in the most progressive circles, and left its mark on a good deal of the music written during the 'twenties and early 'thirties. It influenced Stravinsky for a time, and it would not perhaps be fanciful to see a connection between the sort of objective, impersonal music of

Satie and the mechanistic de-humanised productions of the
Gebrauchsmusik school. Be that as it may, in *Socrate* Satie
achieved something that no one hitherto had attempted in
music—the weaving of a kind of tapestry of sound to carry a long,
melodic narration entrusted to four different voices, succeeding
one another like runners in a relay race. It was characteristic of
the man that he should have set himself a task so difficult as that
of providing a musical setting for passages from the Dialogues of
Plato. Yet we feel the intuition which guided him in the choice
of his text was infallibly right. Who else could have been trusted
not to overlay the beauties of the text with a too elaborate or
pretentious mantle of notes? Who else would have been content
to approach with such humility this self-imposed task which
Satie himself described as 'an act of piety, an artist's dream, a
humble homage'? The very modesty and restraint of the means
which Satie allows himself create, it is true, a certain impression
of monotony (perhaps most noticeable in the version with piano
accompaniment) but at the same time the style in which
Socrate is written makes great demands upon the singers. For
there is no opportunity at all for vocal display, and yet the in-
terpreters must 'feel' intensely what they are singing. The
listener has to imagine that he is overhearing, as it were, someone reading aloud, the voice rising and falling on a thin melodic
line, absolutely and closely wedded to the wonderfully simple
and poignant prose of the narration. It is solitary music and
could only have been conceived by a mind sensitive to beauty,
but dwelling in a sort of spiritual stratosphere, in a rarefied
isolation. As has been well said,[22] 'this music has no human
population; the balanced phrases unfold infinitely in an empty
room of which the walls are built of parallel mirrors. There is
nothing to indicate the passing of time; it is a very tiny world,
but it is self-reflected into infinity'.

This 'timelessness' can also be construed in another sense, that
of 'agelessness'. For the work is so completely impersonal and
objective and so closely reflects the feeling of the Greek original
(though there is nothing specifically 'Greek' about the music,
nor did Satie aim at anything of the kind) that it could never be
a 'period' piece, any more than Plato's Dialogues could be.

It has been said that Satie was instinctively drawn to Plato
because he saw in Socrates a reflection of himself. Both were
ironists, both had questing, inquisitive, 'gad-fly' dispositions,

[22]See W. H. Mellers: 'Erik Satie and Contemporary Music', *Studies in Contemporary Music*, Dobson, 1948.

both concealed under a mocking exterior a profound disillusionment; both, in their different ways, were thinkers pursuing a
lonely path, obstinate in their convictions and undeterred by the
incomprehension and even hostility of their fellow-men. And if
Socrates was not indifferent to the wayward charm and eccentric
brilliance of the Athenian Alcibiades, nor did Satie escape altogether the influence of that other *enfant terrible* of genius, the
Parisian Jean Cocteau . . . The parallel should not be laboured,
but there is enough resemblance between the two personalities
to make a reference to it, with obvious reservations, permissible.

At any rate Satie had no illusions about the difficulty of the
task he had set himself, and approached it with considerable
misgivings and a proper respect for the nobility and beauty of
the text which he felt hardly needed the addition of music. Had
he felt otherwise, *Socrate* could not have been the masterpiece it
is. He made his own selection from the rather frigid and stilted
translation by Victor Cousin of the *Symposium*, the *Phaedrus* and
Phaedo with skill and taste, and in his setting of the immortal
description of the Death of Socrates, especially, he rose to
greater heights than ever before. Abjuring all embellishments,
banishing theatricality and rhetoric, he allows the beautiful
narration to stand out in clear relief; the poignancy of the end
is achieved by an almost miraculous simplicity of means, the
only descriptive touch being the knell-like chords and drum-
beats on a reiterated pedal which, with great sobriety and tragic
effect, underline the death of one whom Plato called (through
the mouth of Phaedo) 'the wisest and justest and best of all the
men whom I have ever known'.

Socrate had its first performance at a concert of the Société
Nationale in Paris in January 1920. It was met, naturally, with
incomprehension, and a section of the audience tittered.
'Strange, is it not'? was Satie's only comment at the time; but
he had foreseen only too clearly what was likely to happen, and
before the *première* he published a warning, in his old, truculent
style, couched in these terms: 'Those who are unable to understand are requested by me to adopt an attitude of complete
submission and inferiority'.

This kind of thing was certainly not likely to please the critics,
and Jean Marnold even went so far as to declare the work to be a
monument of 'impotence and complete nullity'. Charles
Koechlin, on the other hand, discerned genius in *Socrate*, and
Alfred Cortot in a later valuation of Satie's work called it a work
of a 'high aesthetic order'. The composer himself confessed he

57

had put into it 'the best he had in him' and we must believe him. His biographer, P. D. Templier, raises an interesting point in this connection when he suggests that the work might never have been written if Debussy had still been alive, and that it was only after the death of his old friend and protector that Satie dared to reveal his true nature and the full extent of his powers and take the risk of being judged on his merits as a wholly serious composer. This seems highly probable, and provides an interesting explanation of the sort of diffidence and atmosphere of mystification with which Satie had hitherto surrounded himself and his music, as if fearing to be taken too seriously, and possibly found wanting, by those whose judgement he valued most highly. For although in his eyes Debussy and Ravel and their school were almost 'old-fashioned' and *passé* (he referred to them half-affectionately, half-mockingly as *les périmés*—the 'outworn ones') yet there is no doubt that for Debussy at least Satie secretly felt both respect and admiration, and shrank from seeming to be in any way his rival—knowing, as he did, his own limitations.[23] But this attitude was bound to set up inhibitions in Satie; in fact it literally 'cramped his style'. And so M. Templier is perhaps right when he suggests that Debussy's disappearance meant for Satie a kind of 'liberation' of which the first happy effects were manifested in this work into which he put 'the best of himself'— *Socrate.*

[23]In an article entitled 'Les Périmés' published in the *Les Feuilles Libres* (March 1923) Satie made his position clear. In his view the 'périmés' were above all the *imitators* of Debussy—the 'sous-Debussystes' as he called them. 'Do not imagine', he wrote, 'that I have lost an inch of my affection for my regretted and distinguished friend Debussy, or a particle of my admiration for his dear and delightful memory. No. But I can only laugh at those who today coolly speak "in his name" and think they have inherited his splendid genius, his exquisite "manner". . . . Personally I was *very closely* associated with the fight Debussy had to put up against those very same nonentities ("demi-personnages") who are now praising him, stupidly, posing as his friends, and just "discovering" him today. It is perhaps regrettable that they did not do so when my eminent friend was going through a difficult and painful period in his life. And yet many of these "late admirers" had attained at that time more than the age of reason. They might have seen clearly then—even without a magnifying glass or spectacles. Only . . . then . . . "one didn't know that . . ." You understand? For these cautious and cunning folk are not heroes—why should they be, after all? Quite so. And so they waited to see what would happen, until they could be quite sure. . . . Now the situation in which these "out-worn" gentle-men find themselves is sufficiently comic. Their artistic "journey" can only end badly. They embarked on an old ship, "modern style", leaking up to the mast-heads. They write "richly" in an incredibly gilded and would-be luxuriant style— as false as a false nose. Their bad taste assails the eye, the ears, even the shins of the least intelligent obesrver. This bad taste relegates them to the very slums of Art, where all they can do is to stagnate like a lot of old nuts, ignored by everyone and cut off from Life. Even the Sun shrugs his age-old and torrid shoulders at their pretentious and insipid cooings, and firmly refuses to shed light upon them—even gas-light. . . .'

58

Chapter V

1920—1925

'Musique d'ameublement'; *the ballets* 'Mercure' *and* 'Relâche'; *the* 'Ecole d'Arcueil '; *last days.*

THE LAST FIVE YEARS of his life were for Satie in some ways the most agitated. They were also among the most fertile of his career and witnessed the production of several key works which reveal the innovator and pioneer that he was now recognised to be in yet another phase of his versatile and chameleonic evolution. For *Socrate* was by no means his swan song. Nor did he attempt another work of such a purely serious character again. From now on he was to become increasingly absorbed in the theatre, writing two more ballets, which created quite as great a stir as *Parade,* as well as launching his famous 'musique d'ameublement'. He had now abandoned the piano, after writing for it the *Five Nocturnes* of 1919, which incidentally are among the best things he ever did and comparable in style and feeling to *Socrate* which was composed about the same time. In complete contrast to the latter work and immediately succeeding it came the *Trois Petites Pièces Montées* (illustrating the childhood of Rabelais's Pantagruel) for small orchestra written in a rumbustious 'popular' vein with humorous wind effects and full of verve and crude high spirits—the kind of 'street-corner' music, in fact, which the 'Six' were writing about that time. In the same year (1920) Satie wrote a piece of frankly music-hall character for Mlle Caryathis, a dancer who was then appearing at the Théâtre des Champs-Elysées. It was called *La Belle Excentrique* and is a throw-back to his Montmartre café-concert period not exempt from a certain vulgarity, which was of course intentional. The sub-titles, too, are reminiscent of the earlier humoristic period: e.g., 'Marche Franco-Lunaire,' 'Valse du mystérieux baiser dans l'oeil', 'Can-can Grand Mondain', etc., and the whole thing may be considered as a *pièce d'occasion* which Satie took the opportunity of turning into an amusing parody of music-hall clichés. Of the *Quatre Petites Mélodies,* one of the least-known of his four sets of songs, which were written at this time, it is noteworthy that the 'Elegy' was dedicated to the memory of Claude Debussy and published separately in a special number of the *Revue Musicale* entitled *Tombeau de Debussy*

59

to which most of the leading French composers had been invited to contribute. Satie's dedication ran as follows: 'In memory of an admiring and happy (douce) friendship of thirty years'.

The term 'musique d'ameublement' ('furnishing music') which can be applied to many of the later, or 'third period' works, originated in a statement made by Matisse who declared that he dreamed of an art without any distracting subject-matter which might be compared to an easy-chair ('. . . quelque chose d'analogue à un bon fauteuil').

Now, although *Socrate* is usually cited as an outstanding example of this idea translated in terms of music, it was not until after its first performance that the 'musique d'ameublement' was officially designated and introduced to the public under that name. The occasion was a picture exhibition held at the Galérie Barbazanges in the Faubourg St Honoré on March 8, 1920, when music specially composed by Satie for a play by Max Jacob was performed in the gallery while people were looking at the pictures. It was played by a little band of instruments consisting of a piano, three clarinets and a trombone and introduced by M. Pierre Bertin in the following terms:

We present for the first time, under the supervision of MM. Erik Satie and Darius Milhaud and directed by M. Delgrange, 'furnishing music' to be played during the entr'actes. We beg you to take no notice of it and to behave during the entr'actes as if the music did not exist. This music . . . . claims to make its contribution to life in the same way as a private conversation, a picture, or the chair on which you may or may not be seated. . . . .

Unfortunately the audience disregarded these instructions and kept silent while the music was being played, to the great annoyance of Satie who went about urging people to talk and make a noise, as the music, which consisted of fragments of popular refrains from *Mignon* and the *Danse Macabre* and isolated phrases repeated over and over again, like the pattern of wallpaper, was meant strictly to be nothing more than a background and was not intended to attract attention in any way.

People looked upon the whole thing as a joke; but in reality it was more than that, being based on a theory of listening particularly applicable to the cinema where, indeed, it was later to attain its full significance, as when Satie wrote the film music for the *Entr'acte* in the Surrealist ballet *Relâche*. Here the action on the screen is accompanied by musical phrases cut, as it were, into lengths, constantly repeated and juxtaposed without any attempt at illustration and quite dissociated from the meaning of the images presented to the eye. The role of the music in fact is deliberately confined to underlining the action indirectly without calling attention to itself so that the spectator is free to concentrate on the visual image, which is thus presented to him framed, as it were, by musical patterns which perform much the same unobtrusive function as a picture-frame does for the picture it encloses. Once again Satie had hit upon an entirely 'new' technique, the importance of which it would seem that composers writing for the films today have tended rather surprisingly to overlook.

The ballet *Relâche* for which Satie wrote all the music, as well as this *Entr'acte Cinématographique*, was written in 1924, the year before he died, and followed at a short interval another ballet of a different but equally revolutionary kind, *Mercure*. Both these works have a very important place in his *œuvre* and it is time now to give some account of them.

In the summer of 1924 Count Etienne de Beaumont organised a season of ballets and 'advanced' theatrical productions at the Cigale Theatre in Montmartre under the comprehensive title of *Soirées de Paris*. Among those from whom he commissioned new works for production during the season was Satie who was invited to write a ballet in collaboration with Picasso and Massine. The result was *Mercure*—the adventures of Mercury —described as 'poses plastiques'. Picasso devised entrancing costumes and sets, and Satie supplied music which once more disconcerted both his former admirers (some at least) and his habitual detractors. On the first night, for reasons which now appear obscure, the Surrealists and others created such a disturbance that the curtain had to be lowered in the middle of the performance and rival factions in the audience nearly came to blows. Picasso incurred the displeasure of his followers for allowing himself to be mixed up in what people took to be a studio farce; and Satie, as usual, was reviled and attacked on all sides. It was *Parade* all over again. The music was in the old 'circus-music-hall' style, especially as regards the instrumentation, but the treatment was if anything almost academic. Satie declared that his music was exactly fitted to express what the authors of the ballet had in mind, and that his aim was to produce a score which although not a mere imitation of the music-hall orchestra would yet incorporate rhythms which had a special association with the play-house. It has been said that *Mercure* was a painter's ballet, the chief honours going to Picasso, but it is difficult to conceive it with any other music than Satie's which

61

has an extraordinary appropriateness which contributed perhaps not a little to the effect of Picasso's designs.

It is perhaps desirable at this point to open a parenthesis in order to give some idea of the aesthetic background against which the works of Satie's last period have to be considered. When *Parade* was produced in 1917 the 'Dada' movement in the arts had just been born. The 1914 war had engendered a feeling of hopelessness and despair among artists throughout Europe. It seemed as if all known values were in process of being destroyed, that civilisation and all that it implied in the way of culture and decency and human significance was doomed to destruction, and that in consequence art and literature were meaningless. Everything therefore that belonged to these spheres of human activity and human intelligence would have to be thrown back into the melting pot before a new spirit and a new consciousness could arise that would be able to function on another plane altogether, and through which mankind would be enabled to adjust itself to a changed world and new modes of existence, both moral and material, as unlike those it had known before the cataclysm as a butterfly is unlike the chrysalis from which it so surprisingly emerges. And so everything that had had meaning and beauty before would have to be destroyed, and man's spiritual and mental evolution arrested, and thrust back, if only for a while, into the dark cocoon of submerged consciousness. That was what Dada was intended to express—an utter nihilism in the domain of the intellect and the arts. 'It was', said a writer in *Time*[24] (December 14, 1936) 'a conscious attack on reason, a negation of everything, the loudest and silliest expression of post-war cynicism'.

The actual founder of Dada was Tristan Tzara, the Rumanian poet and artist, who claims to have launched the movement from a café in Zürich on February 8th, 1916. In France and in Germany it found a certain number of adherents in the post-war years, among whom were a group of brilliant young men such as André Breton, Paul Eluard, Louis Aragon, Philippe Soupault, and the painters Hans Arp and Max Ernst. It is not, then, surprising that it was in 1921 that Pierre Bertin conceived the idea of producing Satie's *Le Piège de Méduse* which, although written eight years earlier, had as we have already seen, so strikingly anticipated Dada. But by 1922 Dada had died out, and was succeeded by Surrealism which was to prove a far more formidable, fertile and permanent influence which has left its

[24]Quoted by N. Slominsky in *Music since 1900*, p. 166.

mark on an appreciable proportion of the artistic and literary output of the last quarter of a century, and is still a force to be reckoned with, especially in painting.

In the early 'twenties, then, when Satie was at last being recognised as a pioneer and considered as belonging definitely to the *avant-garde*, this meant that in the eyes of the public and the critics he was more or less vaguely associated with Cubism (*Parade*), Dadaism (*Le Piège de Médusé*), Surrealism or whatever other '-ism' may have been fashionable at the time. The fact is that, although acutely conscious of all these 'movements' (to which he had perhaps unconsciously been contributing all through his career) Satie belonged to none of them. In this, he was like Picasso and Stravinsky, who have never allowed themselves to be labelled. At the same time he was on the fringe of all that was going on in these spheres and it is not to be wondered at that after *Mercure* he was approached by his Surrealist friends and invited to collaborate with them in what was described as a 'ballet instantanéiste'. Francis Picabia and Marcel Duchamp were perhaps not officially members of the group, but might be described as 'near-Surrealists'; at all events their ballet *Relâche* was to all intents and purposes Surrealist, if not Dada. Satie, who was now 58, was charmed at the novelty and inconsequentiality of Picabia's scenario, and enthusiastically set about composing the music for it. The choreography was in the hands of Jean Borlin and his Swedish Ballet (the creators, among other things, of Milhaud's *La Création du Monde*) and there was an important cinematographic episode, devised and directed by René Clair, which some enterprising film company ought to disinter and exhibit for the joy and edification of a generation which knows nothing of the early experimental work, on Surrealist lines, of the real pioneers in the art of the cinema, 'Tenth Muse'. . . .

Mention has already been made of the music which Satie wrote for this *Entr'acte cinématographique*, thereby inventing something entirely new and original in this genre. The music for the ballet proper, or rather pantomime, was based on popular tunes which Satie selected for their 'evocative' qualities as being most in keeping with the 'unbuttoned' nature of the scenario. He foresaw the kind of criticism likely to be directed against him for adopting this procedure, and retaliated in advance with one of his aggressive declarations—'. . . The timid folk and the "moralists" blame me for making use of these tunes. I am not interested in the opinions of such people. . . . The reactionary

63

"calves' heads" will fulminate . . . Peuh!—I only admit one judge: the public. It will recognise these tunes and won't be at all shocked to hear them. Isn't the public "human"? . . . I would not wish to make a lobster blush—or even an egg. . . . Let those who are afraid of these "evocations" keep away. I should be ashamed to trouble their serene innocence. . . . I am too good-natured to want to displease them'.

This attitude was quite in keeping with the whole tone of the ballet which was intended to shock and irritate the Parisians; its authors described it as being directed against 'the pretentious absurdities of the theatre', and as representing 'life as I like it, life without a tomorrow, the life of today—everything for to-day, nothing for yesterday, nothing for tomorrow.' One of Picabia's slogans was 'down with all forms of academicism'; another, 'Art becomes a pleasure'. Everything possible was done to provoke and irritate the public; under Picabia's portrait on the programme were the words: 'I would rather hear them pro-testing than applauding'; and posters were exhibited on the stage during the performance announcing, for example, 'Erik Satie is the greatest musician in the world'; or, 'If you are not satisfied, the box-office will sell you a whistle for a couple of bob'. The authors even appeared on the stage crowded into a 'baby' 5 H.P. car. . . . And to crown all, after all Paris had been worked up into a state of excitement and eager expectation by means of a sensational advance publicity, when the fashionable audience arrived for the much-advertised first night, they found the theatre in darkness and the doors closed. Naturally everyone concluded that they were the victims of a hoax; the posters out-side the theatre bearing the title of the piece, *Relâche*, spoke only too truthfully; the authors had scored their first success.[25] However, three days later the show was presented, and had a mixed reception. It was crazy, it was fantastic, it was grotesque —but it was certainly amusing and quite unlike anything ever seen on the Parisian stage before. In the film there were shots of Satie firing a cannon on the roof of the Théâtre des Champs-Elysées, and clambering over the gargoyles on Notre-Dame; and many people felt that this time he had gone too far. Was this the composer of the grave and beautiful *Socrate?*—the author of those limpid and appealing *Gymnopédies* which had won the admiration of the *Périmés* he now affected to despise? How could he have lent himself to such clownings, and become the associate

[25]'Relâche' is the regular term employed in France to indicate that a theatre is closed and that there will be no performance.

Erik Satie *by Francis Picabia*

a mon cher Erik Satie
Jean Cocteau
1920

Erik Satie *by Jean Cocteau*

of irresponsible *farceurs* such as Picabia and his friends had shown themselves to be? It was feelings such as these that prompted one critic, after *Relâche*, to pen an article which he entitled: 'Adieu Satie . . .'

The composer was hurt by what he considered the defection of his friends, although of course he cared nothing for the reactions of the public. In any case he was to write no more. He was by this time a sick man, and from now until his death, apart from a short lecture tour in Belgium which he undertook in 1924, he appeared no more in public.

But it was characteristic of the man that his last works should have been of 'futuristic' tendencies, thus bearing witness to his ever-green appetite for *'l'esprit nouveau'*. His sympathies were always with the young, and his own spirit remained youthful to the last. 'I have always trusted youth', he declared apropos of the group of young composers whom he sponsored at the end of his life—the four young men who took the title of 'Ecole d'Arcueil, as a mark of their admiration for the 'Bon Maître' who had made that suburb famous. 'And up to now I have not been disappointed. Our epoch is favourable to youth. But let them beware—their youth will expose them to attack. . . . One need not be very astute to notice that people of a certain age always talk about their "experience". . . . It is very good of them. . . . But one ought, all the same, to be sure that they have really had any experience. . . . Human memory is very short. . . . is one not accustomed, whenever the weather behaves in an unusual way, to hear people say: "There's been nothing like this within living memory" . . I'm quite ready to believe them. But don't let them talk to me too much about their "experience" . . . their flair—I know them—I know them only too well. . . . And so these young men will be blamed because they are young. I wrote my *Sarabandes* at the age of 21, in 1887; the *Gymnopédies* when I was 22 in 1888. These are the only works which my detractors—those over the age of fifty, of course—admire. To be logical, they ought to like the works of my maturity . . . but no . . .'

It was in such terms, which reflect the disillusionment of one who all his life had remained young in spirit and more than abreast of the times in which he lived, but without ever winning the recognition accorded to lesser men—it was in such terms that Satie at the end of his life expressed, rather touchingly, his faith in the young men who now came forward as his disciples. Their names were Roger Désormière, Henri Cliquet-Pleyel, Maxime Jacob, and Henri Sauguet. Of these the first two, now dead, did acquire some measure of fame as conductor and composer, respectively; Maxime Jacob is now a Benedictine monk, still composing, while Henri Sauguet is one of the best known composers of his generation.

It was Darius Milhaud who brought these young men to Satie in 1923, and it was he, their 'Bon Maître', who guided their first steps, encouraged them and made their names known to the public. The 'École d'Arcueil' may not seem very important to us today, as we look back upon those distant years, the early 'twenties; but it serves at least to remind us that Erik Satie's generous and kindly championship of youth and the wisdom of his teaching did not go wholly unrewarded. As Cocteau put it in his tribute to the 'solitary old man of Arcueil', written after his death: 'Satie, who was supposed to have dried up, blossomed out with flowers and fruit; his candid branches scented and nourished a younger generation wearied with too much artificiality'.

He died on July 1st, 1925, in the Hôpital St. Joseph, after a lingering illness which lasted for six months. He saw no one but a few of his most faithful friends, and was courageous until the end. Nor did his sense of impish humour desert him even in those last days. It has been recorded by one who was with him on his death-bed that he bore everything 'sans jamais cesser tout-à-fait de sourire'. He died, in fact, as he had lived—'without ever quite ceasing to smile'.

Part Two: The Works

Chapter VI

The Piano Music

SATIE MIGHT BE DESCRIBED as a fairly prolific composer, although he never essayed any really large-scale work.

His compositions fall into three main categories: Piano Music: Songs; Music for the Stage—the latter comprising operettas and ballets. He left no purely symphonic music, and the ballets and incidental stage music contain practically all that he wrote for full orchestra. As the piano works are the most voluminous and contain the essence of his peculiar genius, they may fittingly be considered first.

Alfred Cortot in his study of Satie's pianistic writings published in the *Revue Musicale* of April 1938, points out that the composer's œuvre, like Beethoven's (he adds: '*et révérence parler*') may be divided into three distinct periods. The first, from 1886 to 1895, he calls 'the period of mysticism and medieval influences'; the second, from 1897 to 1915, the period of 'mystification' and eccentricity; the third, from 1916 to 1925 (the year of Satie's death), the period of the 'musique d'ameublement'. The last decade incidentally also saw the production of all Satie's major works for the stage.

The division is a convenient one and corresponds more or less accurately to the rhythm of the composer's evolution.

The first thing that strikes one in examining the compositions of the first period is that they contain in them the germs of all subsequent developments. Satie was only twenty-one when he wrote the now famous *Sarabandes* whose harmonies sounded so strangely daring in 1887 to ears accustomed to the suavities of Massenet and Gounod. At this time, it must be remembered,

67

Debussy was still in his student stage; five years were to elapse before his new sonorities were made manifest in the *Prélude à l'Après-midi d'un Faune,* and six before the String Quartet ushered in the music of the future—of the twentieth century. As yet Debussy had written nothing for piano solo, and the innovations that Fauré was beginning to introduce so discreetly into the accepted harmonic language of the period were so well camouflaged as to be almost imperceptible except to the keenest observers. Indeed the only really 'revolutionary' composer at that time who might have an equal claim with Satie to be considered as an innovator was Emmanuel Chabrier. French critics, for example, have observed that the score of *Le Roi Malgré Lui,* which also dates from 1887, contains certain harmonic progressions, notably successions of unresolved chords of the ninth, very similar to those employed by Satie in his *Sarabandes.* Compare, for example, this passage from Chabrier's operetta:

with this from the third *Sarabande*:

This music is also characterised by its grave, liturgical character and by the marching blocks of chords which seem to anticipate the technique of the later mystical works, such as the *Fils des Etoiles* Preludes (1891) and the *Prélude de la Porte Héroïque du Ciel* (1894).

But oddly enough, the very next year Satie was to write his three *Gymnopédies* which seem to spring from an entirely different aesthetic. In them he foreshadowed the new linear technique which he was to develop in later years when he had abandoned the modal style of the works of his mystic period. In contrast to the rather heavy, a-rhythmic and static harmonies which characterise the latter, in the *Gymnopédies* a slender, undulating melodic line is traced thinly over a rocking 'pedal' bass of shifting, delicately dissonant chords. The harmonic texture, modal in character, especially in the final cadences, is light and transparent; and the melody seems to have a strange aerial quality as if traced by floating gossamer threads suspended between earth and sky. Like the *Sarabandes* which preceded them, the *Gymnopédies* are three in number—each one representing a different 'facet', as it were, of the basic idea which gives them unity but of which nevertheless each *Gymnopédie* supplies a variant.

This 'Trinitarian' obsession was a peculiarity of Satie's and is manifested over and over again in his works which are frequently conceived as groups of three. Thus in addition to the works already mentioned the following pieces are all in sets of three: *Gnossiennes; Heures séculaires et instantanées; Croquis et agaceries d'un Gros Bonhomme en bois; Embryons desséchés; Chapitres tournés en tous sens; Enfantillages pittoresques;* etc., while *Socrate* is also composed of three sections based on three different Dialogues of Plato. But while this grouping does not invariably indicate an attempt on the part of the composer to present a central musical idea from more than one angle, as a sculptor presents his work so that it can be viewed from every side, in the case of the *Gymnopédies*, as in the *Sarabandes* and *Gnossiennes*, this is precisely what Satie was aiming to do. Let us see how he has succeeded in the three *Gymnopédies* in presenting us with three different views of his edifice while preserving the basic unity which underlies all three variants.

Here are the opening bars of Nos. I, II, and III:

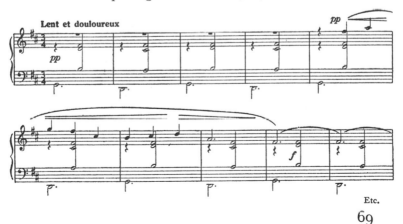

Etc.

And here are the final cadences of each:

Although Debussy paid Satie the compliment of orchestrating the 1st and 3rd *Gymnopédies*, it must be admitted that in so doing he partially destroyed their essential character. The clear outlines and transparent texture are in fact obscured in a sort of impressionistic mist; the soft brush-work of the painter has blurred the etcher's delicate but incisive line. Nevertheless that kindly and disinterested act on Debussy's part has certainly added prestige to the modest *Gymnopédies* and has been the means of making them more widely known.[26] Today their beauty seems as fresh as ever, and their originality outstanding —especially when one remembers the date of their composition. As to whether or not their title is intended to have any pictorial significance is not altogether clear; it seems probable however that Satie (a great specialist in unusual titles) intended to suggest (perhaps with some fresco by Puvis de Chavannes, a painter he admired greatly, in mind) the tracing of some graceful arabesque by naked boys dancing under an early-morning Grecian sky. And to express this he invented a new word, apparently derived from the Greek word γυμνοπαιδιαι[27]. It has also been stated that they were inspired by a reading of Flaubert's *Salammbô*. A similar train of thought probably suggested to him the title *Gnossiennes* which he gave to his next piano pieces—again a set of three—which appeared in 1890. Here there would seem to be some sort of vague allusion to the palace of Knossos in Crete, the scene of the legend of Ariadne and the Minotaur—although the music is entirely non-pictorial and abstract.

The three *Gnossiennes* are the first pieces to be written in bar-less notation, without either key or time signature; here also appear for the first time the humoristic indications written in over the music—a device which the composer was to use so extensively in later years. 'Ouvrez la tête' commands the com-

[26]No. 3 can be heard in the orchestral version on H.M.V. Debussy orchestrated this one first, and it is accordingly No. 1 in the orchestral version.

[27]A yearly festival, mentioned in Herodotus and other authors, in honour of those who fell at Thyrea 'at which naked boys danced and went through gymnastic exercises'.

poser; or again: 'Conseillez-vous soigneusement'; 'Postulez en vous même'. Elsewhere the player is instructed to play 'de manière à obtenir un creux', 'avec étonnement' and 'sur la langue'. But all these odd directions add nothing to the music; nor can they deprive it of its innate expressiveness. All the essential features of Satie's style are already apparent in these pieces—the obstinately repeated melodic phrases, the modal cadences, the basic rhythm firmly established in the bass and persisting to the end. The opening bars of the first *Gnossienne* will serve to illustrate these features:

Coming now to the compositions of the mystic Rose+Croix period, the most significant are the three Preludes to Péladan's *Fils des Etoiles*, the three *Sonneries de la Rose+Croix*, the *Prélude de la Porte Héroïque du Ciel*, and the *Messe des Pauvres*. It seems clear that Satie was at this time in a genuinely religious state of mind; although the composer's sister, Mme Olga Satie-Lafosse, after describing her brother as 'difficult to understand', has expressed the opinion that he was a spiritist rather than a true mystic ('plus spirite que vraiment mystique'). This would no doubt account for the fact that in his Rose+Croix period Satie was under the impression that he was working under the direct guidance of some medieval cleric whose fanatical piety he had inherited from beyond the grave. The works cited were not originally written for piano, with the exception of the *Prélude de la Porte Héroïque du Ciel* (which was not orchestrated until 1912 by M. Roland-Manuel); but since they exist in a piano version made by the composer they have some claim to be considered here. The harmonic idiom was entirely unfamiliar at the time when they were written, and is characterised by unusual progressions of sevenths and ninths, with superimposed fourths alternating with common chords. The rhythm is hesitant, the handling in general seems rather *gauche* and lifeless; but the music, though curiously static, relies for its effect on a certain hypnotic quality induced by repetition and the use of medieval-sounding harmonies. The impression it creates, in a word, is similar to that produced by a piece of rather heavy medieval tapestry. The following extract is from the *Prélude de la Porte Héroïque du Ciel* (1894), dedicated by the composer 'To Myself.'

In the next stage, which was to last for close on twenty years, we see the composer—'Monsieur le Pauvre', as he then styled himself—turning his back on religious inspiration ('musique à genoux') and dedicating himself to the service of a profaner—at times even frivolous—Muse. Satie was now ready to exchange the mantle of the Seer for the cap and bauble of the Jester—though these, again, were really only another form of disguise which he adopted deliberately to shield himself from possibly hostile criticism, which he feared. If the truth were known it is probable that at no time in his life was he absolutely 'sure' of himself, or rather, of his powers; and this gave rise to a certain timidity which led him to commit extravagances. M. Koechlin compares this timidity to that of 'a primitive who has discovered all by himself an unknown world'. For that, in effect, was what Satie had done; by pure intuition he had stumbled upon a hitherto unsuspected 'hinterland' of music which it was his mission in life to develop and reveal to his sceptical and tradition-bound fellow men. The area of this unexplored region was perhaps strictly circumscribed, but it was his discovery, and he was determined to make the most of it, exploit it for all it was worth. And from now on—that is from 1897, the date of the first of the post-mystical piano pieces—he gave himself whole-heartedly to that task.

To these pieces he gave, with characteristic irony, the some-what forbidding title of *Pièces Froides* (*Airs à faire fuir, Danses de travers*).

It goes without saying that the titles are as misleading as they were doubtless intended to be, for nothing could be less frigid or less calculated to inspire flight than these charming airs and dances. Not unlike the *Gnossiennes* in character, but less

73

'static', they represent Satie at his best and I should place them high among his piano writings. Like the *Gymnopédies*, both the Airs and the Dances are grouped in threes, and once again one has to admire the skilful way in which the composer rings the changes on the germ idea. They are written in barless notation in an easy flowing style, eminently pianistic but technically extremely simple; and their texture is crystal-clear. Especially remarkable are the subtle and deliciously unexpected modulations and harmonic progressions managed with an unobtrusive skill worthy of Fauré himself:

and surprising cadences of haunting beauty and simplicity:

Only a born musician of the finest sensibility could have conceived these limpid and so essentially 'musical' pieces which ought to be in the repertory of every pianist who is more interested in music than virtuosity.

Of the remaining pre-Schola Cantorum works much the most important is the piano duet (four hands) *Trois Morceaux en forme de Poire* (1903). The slighter pieces of this period, published posthumously, such as the *Danses Gothiques*, *Les Pantins dansent*, and the four Preludes (*Fête donnée par des Chevaliers Normands en l'Honneur d'une jeune Demoiselle* (11me siècle), the *Prélude d'Eginhard*, and the two *Préludes du Nazaréen*) are less interesting musically, and far less technically accomplished than the *Morceaux* which were written, as we have seen, in answer to Debussy's reproach that Satie's music tended to be lacking in 'form'. In view of the meaning attached in colloquial French to the word 'poire', in the sense of dupe or simpleton, it seems likely that Satie in his choice of a title was slyly poking fun not only at Debussy but at himself—the 'poire'. Actually the work is a superb vindication of his ability not only to write formally but in a vein of almost tender lyricism, à la Schumann, which he here indulges in without any suggestion of tongue in cheek.

I would recommend those who maintain a sceptical attitude towards Satie's claim to be considered a serious composer to study carefully the *Morceaux en forme de Poire*, and to ask themselves whether the passage on the following page, for example, could have been written by anyone who was not a musician to his fingertips.

The full title of this work is:

3 Morceaux en forme de Poire
à 4 mains
avec une Manière de Commencement,
une Prolongation du même,
et un En Plus,
suivi d'une Redite.

The 'Manière de Commencement' is a 'Gnossienne' (not one of the three published as such) which was originally incorporated in the *Fils des Etoiles* music of 1891; the 'En Plus' and the 'Redite' are allusions to the formulae employed by professors at the Conservatoire. All these external trappings and literary allusions are however completely irrelevant; the *Morceaux* have no need of any disguise; they are pure music, now sprightly and gay, now tender and melancholy; always poetical, imaginative, and wholly delightful to the ear.

The years 1905-1908 were for Satie years of study and hard work at the Schola Cantorum, and the only piano pieces written during this time were the little *Prélude en Tapisserie* and the

75

The Piano Music

Passacaille published posthumously. Musically they are unimportant except in so far as they show the first results of the composer's contrapuntal training at the Schola. This was to be increasingly in evidence in the works written between 1908, the year that saw Satie's liberation from the Schola after obtaining his diploma in counterpoint, and 1915. This was a productive period, so far as the piano works are concerned, and a succession of oddly named and grotesquely commentated pieces now poured from his pen. They are of unequal value from a strictly musical point of view, and one is conscious at times of a straining after effect and a desire to be facetious at all costs. It is as if Satie, having gained a reputation for buffoonery, was now determined to exploit that vein to the full—to 'cash in on it' in fact, to borrow a phrase in the common parlance of today. His first composition on leaving the Schola, however, was a serious, even scholastic, suite consisting of Choral, Fugue, and Pastorale published under the title of *Aperçus Désagréables*, which was followed by *En Habit de Cheval*, which also contains a Fugue —and a remarkably ingenious and well-conducted one, even if slightly unorthodox. Both these works are for piano duet, although the second was originally planned for full orchestra.

In a letter to M. Roland-Manuel dated 8.7.1911 Satie reports progress on this composition in the following terms: '*L'Habit de Cheval* fits me pretty well. I am working at it with the necessary calm; it is getting on coldly (il avance froidement) and is turning over very satisfactorily.' And again a month later he describes how he played it to Roussel: 'I played him what you know of *En Habit de Cheval* and the exposition of the other fugue—the "Paper Fugue." The whole thing amused him; he approved this new conception of the fugue—staking everything on the expositions (tout pour les expositions). He likes the little harmonies (les petites harmonies) . . .' Six weeks later Satie again wrote to Roland-Manuel this time with reference to the suggested orchestration of *En Habit de Cheval*: 'My orchestra will consist of 2 flutes, 2 oboes, 1 cor anglais, 2 clarinets, 2 bassoons, 1 sarrusophone, 2 *horns* (*sic*) (an instrument I despise), 2 trumpets (one should never use more), 3 trombones, 1 tuba, 1 bass tuba, percussion and the rest. . . . P.S. d'Indy said about trumpets that three means the end of the world.'

The *Véritables Préludes Flasques* (*pour un chien*) (the 'Flabby Preludes'), 1912, belie their name completely, being, in reality, bony rather than flabby, and severely contrapuntal in style. The three pieces—another trinity—which compose the set are

77

entitled (1) 'Sévère Réprimande'; (2) 'Seul à la maison'; (3) 'On joue'. The music is dry and terse, written for the most part in an austere two-part harmony in which Satie shows considerable ingenuity. The only attempt at humour is in the mock-Latin directions; *corpulentus, caeremoniosus, substantialis,* etc., which supply an additional touch of monkish scholasticism. It is perhaps not generally known that Satie destroyed the original version of the *Préludes Flasques* (he announced this in a letter to M. Roland-Manuel dated 8.8.1912) and re-wrote them under the title, which they now bear, of *Véritables Préludes Flasques.* They were originally submitted to Durand, but having been rejected by that firm were accepted and published by E. Demets. The composer was delighted when Durand expressed his willingness to read them; but deeply offended by his rejection of the MS. Commenting on this scornfully in a letter to M. Roland-Manuel, he writes: 'M. Durand talks about his *customers* who would not care to possess my work . . . that is quite possible . . .'

The *Descriptions Automatiques* which appeared in 1913 marked the beginning of the series of 'clowning' pieces in which the part played by the verbal commentary and musical parodies and allusions becomes increasingly important.

Thus in *Sur un Vaisseau*, the popular song 'Maman, les petits bateaux' is evoked; and in *Sur la Lanterne* there is an allusion to a popular music-hall song of the day, but introduced in such a way as to appear to grow inevitably out of the initial theme. But it is in the *Embryons Desséchés* of the same year (1913) that the composer's fantasy bubbles up to a new high level. Here the music is supposed to portray the 'embryos' of three marine creatures correctly described by their scientific names but depicted in nonsensical terms recalling the manner of Edward Lear.

The first of these creations is called *Holothurie* and is thus introduced: 'Ignorant people call it a "sea cucumber". The Holothurie usually climbs about on stones or rocks. Like the cat, this animal purrs; moreover it spins a kind of moist silk. It appears to be inconvenienced by the action of light. I once observed a Holothurie in the Bay of St. Malo'. Then follows a brisk pianistic exercise (introducing a deformation of the song tune 'Mon Rocher de St Malo') interspersed with droll ironic comments and directions to the player of which the most famous is the instruction to play 'like a nightingale with toothache'. The writing is in bare two-part harmony and the piece ends with reiterated common chords of G major *ff* up and down the keyboard marked 'grandiose'—an evident parody of some of the more emphatic closing perorations of the great symphonists. . . . The second Embryon is an *Edriophthalma*. These are 'crustaceans with sessile eyes, i.e., without stalks and immovable. By nature of a very sad disposition, these crustaceans live, in retirement from the world, in holes pierced in the cliffs'. These mournful creatures are appropriately provided with funereal music which soon turns into a parody of Chopin's Funeral March, introduced textually as a 'quotation from the celebrated Mazurka of Schubert'.

Number Three is dedicated to the *Podophthalma*—'crustaceans whose eyes are placed on mobile stalks. They are skilful and tireless hunters, and are found in every sea. The flesh of the Podophthalma is very tasty and good to eat'. Their liveliness is manifested unmistakably in the music allotted to them; the huntsmen's horn is heard as they scamper about; and they pay no heed to the injunction (from *La Mascotte*) 'Ah! n'courez pas comme ça'. This portrait closes, like the first, with a final cadence ('cadence obligée—de l'Auteur') of reiterated chords of F major.

Continuing in the same vein Satie next produced the *Croquis et Agaceries d'un Gros Bonhomme en Bois*—three lively and witty sketches with intent to parody as their titles show: (1) *Tyrolienne Turque* (allusion to Mozart's 'Turkish March'); (2) *Danse Maigre* (*à la manière de ces messieurs*); (3) *Españana* (poking sly fun at Chabrier and Debussy, with passages marked 'Puerta Maillot', 'Plaza Clichy', 'Rue de Madrid', and 'A la disposicion de Usted'). This piece is dedicated to Mme Debussy.

The *Chapitres Tournés en Tous Sens* are again frankly humoristic. First we are introduced to *Celle qui parle trop*—the wife who expresses a desire for a 'hat in massive mahogany', insisting on talking while her husband, after showing 'signs of impatience', admonishes her to the tune of the well-known air 'Ne parle pas, Rose, je t'en supplie'. But the wife continues with inane remarks such as 'Madame Thingummy has an umbrella made of bone', 'Mlle Whats-her-name has married a man as dry as a cuckoo', 'The Concierge has got a pain in her side'—until the unfortunate husband 'dies of exhaustion'—on an unresolved chord of the eleventh.

The second piece in this set is entitled *Le Porteur de grosses pierres* and is introduced with these words: 'He carries them on his back. His expression is cunning and at the same time full of confidence. Small children are amazed at his strength. As we watch him he is carrying an enormous stone, a hundred times as big as himself. (*It is a pumice stone*)'. The joke here lies in the quotation from an operetta by Rip: 'C'est un rien, un souffle, un rien . . .' In the third and last of the *Chapitres Tournés en Tous Sens* (dedicated to Mme Claude Debussy) entitled *Regrets des En-fermés* Satie introduces the well-known air 'Nous n'irons plus au bois' which had been used with such effect in Debussy's *Jardins sous la pluie*. Satie must have attached considerable importance to these pieces, since he writes on 16th September 1913, to M. Roland-Manuel: 'I have just completed the *Chapitres Tournés en Tous Sens*. I consider this a great triumph.'

More detective work is expected from the listener who is confronted with *Vieux Sequins et Vieilles Cuirasses*, the first of the 1914 piano pieces, in which Gounod, Le Roi Dagobert, and 'Malbrouck s'en va-t-en guerre' are all involved. To the year 1913 also belong the three sets of pieces for children: *Menus Propos Enfantins; Enfantillages Pittoresques; Pecadilles Importunes*. Less sophisticated than *Children's Corner*, these are real children's pieces, simple to play and likely to appeal to an audience with which Satie was in special sympathy.

But with the next set of pieces—bearing the enigmatic title of *Heures Séculaires et Instantanées*—Satie breaks new ground. Here for the first time the isolated verbal quips and sallies are replaced by a kind of recitation or monologue, which is an integral part of the composition. This is no longer a running commentary, arbitrarily superimposed and often irrelevant to the music it accompanies; it is a definite narration, of grotesque inspiration, which the music is there to illustrate. And it is here that Satie issued his dire warning to the performer on no account to read the text out loud—the significance of which has already been discussed in Chapter Three. The *Heures Séculaires*—(there are three of them—yet another example of Satie's mania for ternary grouping) are prefaced in the score in these words: 'To Sir William Grant-Plumot I dedicate agreeably this work. Up to now two personalities have surprised me: Louis XI and Sir William—the first by the strangeness of his good humour (bonhomie); the second by his continual immobility. It is an honour for me to pronounce here the names of Louis XI and of Sir William Grant-Plumot'. As to the identity of 'Sir William' no clue is provided.

The first piece is entitled *Obstacles Vénimeux* and the narration is as follows: 'This vast portion of the globe has only one inhabitant—a negro. He is so bored he is ready to die of laughing. The shade of the thousand-year-old trees shows that it is

9.17 a.m. The toads are calling each other by their family names. In order to think better the negro holds his cerebellum with his right hand, with the fingers spread out. From a distance he resembles a distinguished physiologist. Four anonymous snakes fascinate him, hanging to the skirts of his uniform which is rendered shapeless by sorrow and solitude combined. By the edge of the river an old mangrove tree slowly bathes its roots, which are revoltingly dirty. This is not the hour propitious to lovers (l'heure du berger).'

The second sketch, *Crépuscule Matinal (de midi)* has the following text: 'The sun rose early and in a good humour. The heat will be above normal because the weather is prehistoric and inclined to be thundery. The sun is high in the sky—he looks a good sort. . . . But don't let's trust him. Perhaps he is going to burn up the crops or deliver a mighty stroke—a sun-stroke. Behind the shed an ox is eating itself sick'. ('Slow down politely' is the final direction to the player).

The last of the set bears the extraordinary title of *Affolements Granitiques*, and the words which the music has to illustrate are these: 'The clock in the old deserted village is also going to strike hard—to strike thirteen hours. An antediluvian rainstorm emerges from the clouds of dust. The great mocking trees are tugging at each other's branches, while the rude granite stones push one another about, and don't know where to put themselves so as to be a nuisance. Thirteen hours are about to strike under the general terms of 1 p.m. Alas! this is not legal time'.

In the closing bars Satie indulges in one of his favourite tricks —that of disguising a perfectly ordinary scale passage and a common chord in an outlandish and quite arbitrary notation— thus:

instead of writing simply in the left hand:

followed by:

Each of these pieces is built on perfectly clear and well-defined thematic material, of no great musical interest, perhaps, but none the less by no means formless and not nearly so eccentric as the text that accompanies them. In fact, just as in so many surrealist pictures (and also in the writings and paintings of lunatics) however bizarre the subject may be in itself, the treatment is often quite straightforward and uncompromisingly matter-of-fact, so here the music is quite lacking in the hallucinatory quality of the composer's literary inspiration (inspired nonsense), and incapable by itself of suggesting any images whatever. This seems to throw some light upon the peculiar duality to be observed in Satie's artistic personality—a duality in which opposing parts are played by a classically-minded musician on the one hand and an inveterate *blagueur* on the other. Something of a parallel is to be found in Edward Lear, serious painter and author of the *Nonsense Songs and Stories*—and again in Lewis Carroll, mathematician and clergyman and author of the first surrealist book for children—*Alice in Wonderland*. But whereas Carroll and Lear kept the two sides of themselves distinct (there is no evidence that the former treated the Differential Calculus as a joke or that the latter embellished his landscapes with humorous inscriptions), with Satie it was different. The wag in him was always intruding upon the musician—taking a perverse pleasure in turning the sublime into the ridiculous.

One of the most curious of the works of this period is the set of three waltzes, published under the title of: *Les Trois Valses Distinguées du Précieux Dégôuté* (July 1914). Cortot praises their purely musical content, and points out that this can be savoured without a reference to the humorous text with which again Satie found it necessary to adorn these delightful and ingenious miniature waltzes. Despite the absence of bar lines the stresses, often cunningly displaced, fall naturally into place, and each piece is impeccably 'cut' and shaped. The harmonies, never thicker than three voices, are original as only Satie's harmonies can be, and characteristically dry, though in the second waltz we seem to hear an echo of the early *Gymnopédies*. The 'Precieux Dégôuté' is presented to us under three aspects; first his waist, then his spectacles, then his legs, and each sketch is prefaced by a classical quotation. The first, introducing *Sa Taille*, is from La Bruyère's *Characters*: 'Those who are ready to injure the reputation or the fortune of others rather than lose the opportunity of placing a *bon mot* deserve a humiliating punishment. That has not been said before, but I dare say it.' The second quotation, prefacing *Son Binocle*, is one from Cicero showing how the ban on young men appearing naked in the public baths was an incentive to modesty; and the third, from Cato's *De Re Rustica*, serves to introduce *Ses Jambes* and runs as follows: 'The first duty of the landowner, on arriving at his farm, is to salute his Household Gods; then the same day, if he has time, he must go round his estate and see how the crops are getting on, and what works have been completed and what have not.'

Nothing could be more incongrous than the association of the ideas conveyed in these quotations with those suggested by the music; and to complete the impression of absolute and complete inconsequentiality produced by these arbitrary juxtapositions Satie adds a text of his own which has not the remotest connection with either the music or the passages cited, thus creating a kind of surrealist *montage* of images on three separate entirely disconnected planes.

And so we get a sequence like this:

Waltz No. I : Title : *Sa Taille*—quotation from La Bruyère—composer's commentary as follows: 'He looks at himself. He hums an air of the 15th century. Then he pays himself a compliment of a most discreet nature (tout rempli de mesure). Who would dare to say he is not the handsomest of all? Does he not possess a tender heart? He takes himself by the waist. For him this is an entrancing experience. What will the beautiful Marquise say? She will fight but will be defeated. Yes, Madam. Is it not written?'

Waltz No. II : Title : *Son Binocle*—quotation from Cicero—composer's commentary: 'He cleans them every day. They are silver spectacles with lenses of smoked gold. They were given him by a beautiful lady. Such memories! But . . . our friend is in a profound state of melancholy: he has lost his spectacle case!'

Waltz No. III : Title : *Ses Jambes*—quotation from Cato—composer's commentary: 'They only dance the best dances. They are fine flat legs. In the evenings they are clothed in black. He wants to carry them under his arm. But they slip under him, very sadly. Now they are indignant, in a furious rage. Often he embraces them and puts them round his neck. How good he is

83

to them! He stubbornly refuses to wear gaiters. "A prison!"—
he says'.

Such is the elaborate verbal façade which the composer has
erected round these three waltzes although from a purely
musical point of view they need no commentary at all, and can
very well be listened to as 'abstract' music. There is nothing
'descriptive' about these pieces, nothing in the music that could
suggest a 'programme'; but Satie could not resist the temptation
of dressing them up in a humorous disguise. No doubt he felt
that this was expected of him now; it was, as it were, his 'trade
mark' guaranteeing the authenticity of his products. But at the
same time he evidently took great pains and exercised considerable ingenuity in preparing his texts, and it is difficult to avoid
the conclusion that it was as much for his own private amusement
as for any other reason that he chose to present his music in this
way.

The elegance and clarity of the writing in the *Trois Valses* is
especially noteworthy, as, e.g., in this passage from the first
(*Sa Taille*):

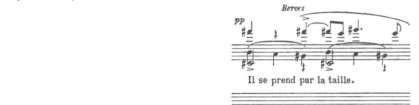

Il se prend par la taille.

C'est pour lui un ravissement.

and again in Number Two (*Son Binocle*) whose nonchalant
rhythm and limpid harmonies recall the *Gymnopédies*:

Il le nettoie tous les jours.

Some passages are frankly bi-tonal:

—a practice which in after years was to be adopted by 'Les Six'; although in 1914, when these pieces were written, it was still something of a novelty.

Before discussing the *Sports et Divertissements*, which are dated 1914, but are in a class apart, a slight departure from strict chronological order is justified in order to include the *Avant-dernières Pensées* (written in 1915) in the group of pieces we have been examining and to which they properly belong. Here again an element of parody is present and a tendency to bi-tonal harmonies, combined with a sort of attenuated lyricism characteristic of the Satie of this period—the whole mixture seasoned, as usual, with a more or less irrelevant verbal commentary. Of the three pieces which make up the set, the first, *Idylle*, is dedicated to Debussy; the second, *Aubade*, to Paul Dukas; and the third, *Méditation*, to Albert Roussel. There seems, however, to be little evidence of any desire to 'imitate' the style of either of these three composers; the pieces are in no sense *à la manière de* . . . , and in spite of their musicality the actual musical content is, as Cortot points out, 'curiously insignificant'.

But with *Sports et Divertissements* we find ourselves on very different ground. These are a set of twenty brilliant little thumbnail sketches of various out-of-door sports and amusements published in an *édition de luxe* in which the original manuscript of Satie, on music-paper ruled with red lines and showing his beautiful calligraphy, is reproduced in facsimile overleaf.

Darius Milhaud considers *Sports et Divertissements* to be one of the most characteristic works of the modern French School; and both Charles Koechlin and Cortot give them high praise, the latter comparing them to the 'Haï-Kaï' and the former to the 'Netzuké' in which the artists and poets of Japan have for so long excelled. Here music and text are indissolubly bound together; both are meant as 'illustrations', and the words are strictly relevant to the subject in hand—unlike those in some of the works we have been examining which have no bearing at all on the music.

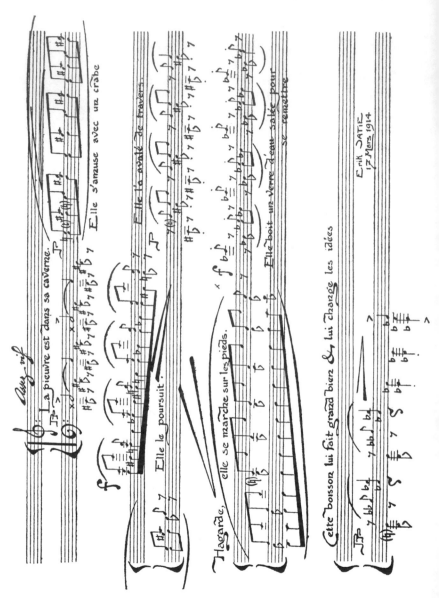

For these are genuine 'sketches'; and although the wit and humour are still there, they no longer belong to that purely illogical and inconsequential world of fantasy uncontrolled which Satie allowed to intrude into so much of his serious work. Here they are deliberately descriptive and employed for a specific purpose.

The story of how *Sports et Divertissements* came to be written is worth relating. The Parisian firm of publishers, Lucien Vogel, were looking for a composer to write music to accompany an album of a score of drawings by an artist called Charles Martin illustrating various sports, and among those approached was Igor Stravinsky. The fee he asked, however, was considered excessive; and it was then that Satie's name was put forward by his friend the composer M. Roland-Manuel. This kindly and disinterested action, however, nearly led to a final rupture in their relations owing to Satie's extraordinarily super-sensitive and unworldly character, For, although the modest fee suggested was far less than that proposed by Stravinsky, to Satie it seemed so enormous that he took offence, imagining that it could only do him harm if he were to ask for such a sum which, moreover, it would have been against his principles to accept. It would have seemed wrong to him to make money out of his music, which he was accustomed to sell to his publishers for sums so trifling that we today can only wonder at his unworldliness. In the end, however, a compromise was reached and a fee small enough to satisfy the composer's peculiar sense of values was agreed, and on March 14th, 1914, Satie started work and wrote the first of these little masterpieces of wit and ironic observation which reveal his genius perhaps more convincingly than any other of his works, with the exception of *Socrate*.

In the Preface he contributed he advises the reader to 'turn the pages of this book with an amiable and smiling hand; for this is a work of fantasy, and does not pretend to be anything else. For those who are dried up and stultified ("les Recroquevillés" et "les Abêtis") I have written a Choral which is serious and respectable. This Choral is a sort of bitter preamble, a kind of austere and unfrivolous introduction. I have put into it everything I know about Boredom. I dedicate this Choral to those who do not like me—and withdraw. Erik Satie.'

In point of fact the Choral is an impressive fragment, and in spite of its brevity (eleven bars, if bar-lines were added), produces an impression of rugged strength and concentrated musical thinking which, though austere, is anything but boring. (Under

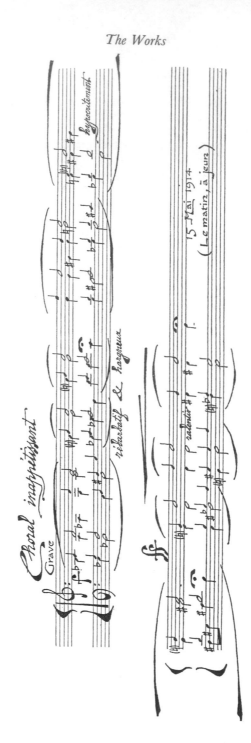

the date the composer characteristically adds: 'In the morning, fasting'.)

The twenty sketches which make up the collection are the following:

La Balançoire (The Swing).
La Chasse (Hunting).
Comédie Italienne (Italian comedy).
La Mariée (The Bride).
Colin-Maillard (Blind Man's Buff).
La Pêche (Fishing).
Yachting
Bain de Mer (Bathing).
Le Carnaval (Carnival).
Le Golf.
La Pieuvre (The Octopus or Squid).
Les Courses (Racing).
Les Quatre Coins (Puss in the Corner).
Pique Nique (Picnic).
Water-Chute.
Le Tango.
Traineau (The Sledge).
Flirt.
Feu d'artifice (Fireworks).
Le Tennis.

All of these are accompanied by a verbal commentary which is sometimes witty and imaginative, sometimes droll, but always amusing and unexpected. This, for example, is how Satie comments on the 'Hunting' sketch: 'Do you hear the rabbit singing? What a voice! The nightingale is in its burrow. The owl is suckling her young. The wild boar is going to get married. As for me, I am shooting down nuts with my gun.'

And now here is *Le Golf* (marked 'exalté'): 'The Colonel is dressed in bright green "Scotch tweed". He is going to be victorious. His "caddie" follows him carrying the "bags". The clouds are astonished. The "holes" are all trembling. The Colonel is there! Watch him preparing to strike: his "club" flies off in little pieces!' In the first bars, by a strange coincidence, Satie seems to have anticipated by some ten years the popular tune 'Tea for Two'.

In 'Blind Man's Buff' Satie with a few delicate strokes of his pen etches in lightly in words and music a miniature sentimental drama, thus: 'Try to catch him, Mademoiselle. He who loves you is very near. How pale he is; his lips are trembling. Are you laughing? He is holding his heart with both hands. But you pass him by without knowing . . .' And suspense and anguish are unforgettably conveyed in the final, questioning chord. But perhaps the most Japanese of all is *La Balançoire* which is indeed a perfect little 'Haï-Kaï' both in words and music:

'It is my heart that is swinging so. It is not feeling dizzy. What small feet it has. Will it want to come back inside my breast again?' And this is how it looks in Satie's exquisite calligraphy—an art which he studied for years while poring over old Gothic manuscripts. (*Reproduced opposite.*)

This is not the place to describe in detail each of these twenty miniatures; from the examples given the reader will be able to form an idea of their extraordinary concision, aptness, acuteness of observation and subtlety of expression. Satie here proves himself an artist of the finest quality, working to a scale which in itself would be a handicap to most writers, let alone musicians, but triumphing over his self-imposed limitations with the virtuosity of a marksman scoring a bull's-eye with each shot. On a miniature range, perhaps; but is artistry a matter of dimensions? For, as M. Koechlin remarks: 'is not a little Japanese ivory worth more than all those official statues which turn our public squares into cities of the dead?' And if anyone thinks (the same writer adds) that these 'trifles' could be easily imitated, 'let him try his hand at something of the kind; he will be surprised. . . .'

It is difficult, indeed, to think of any contemporary composer who could have even attempted to do what Satie accomplished in *Sports et Divertissements* with so sure a touch and such a high measure of success—with the possible exception of Bartók. As it is they remain up to the present unchallenged and unique.

Three years—years of war—were to elapse between the completion of *Sports et Divertissements* and the appearance (in 1917) of Satie's next work for piano solo—the *Sonatine Bureaucratique*. This is an essay in the neo-classic style (in this case in the pianistic style of Clementi) which had already been adumbrated by Debussy in his 'Dr. Gradus ad Parnassum' (*Children's Corner*) and was subsequently exploited to the full by the 'neo-classics' of the nineteen-twenties. Apart from the anecdotal seasoning, already referred to, with which Satie enlivened this little work, the Sonatine is not remarkable musically except as a fairly successful but unexciting pastiche. It was followed two years later by the composer's final *opus* for piano solo—the remarkable set of *Five Nocturnes* composed in 1919. The Nocturnes (planned as a set of six, but uncompleted), occupy a place

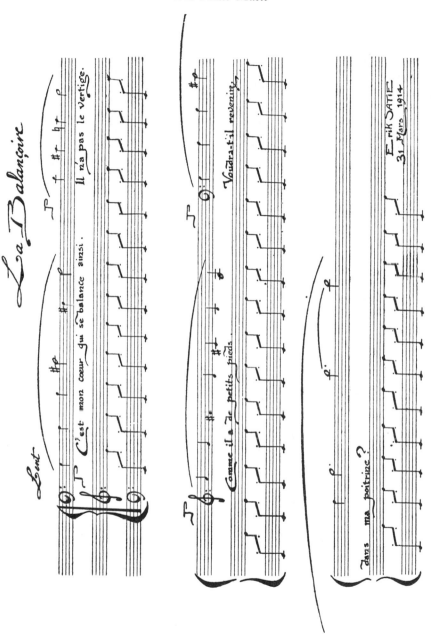

apart in Satie's *œuvre*. In them is contained all the innate 'classicism' that throughout was at the base of Satie's art, but now at its *état pur*, stripped of all the eccentricities and extra-musical adjuncts, the irony and facetiousness that encumbered much of the earlier work. The Nocturnes are in a sense the natural corollary of *Socrate*, which preceded them by a year, and are conceived in the same gravely austere mood. The style is chastened, simplified, uncompromising in its rejection of any sensuous appeal, but the music is strangely impressive in its bleakness and almost inhuman detachment. Harmonically, too, these pieces show a most interesting evolution in Satie's style. As always fifths and fourths form the harmonic keystone; but the progressions proceed, as it were, elliptically, producing an effect of bareness which is almost hallucinatory in its remoteness.

The icy aloofness and completely unromantic emotional atmosphere of these 'Nocturnes' might have appeared incomprehensible to John Field or Frederic Chopin; but from a purely pianistic point of view they are not so very far removed from their nineteenth-century prototype. In this example (from the 4th Nocturne) is there not something Chopinesque about the flowing arpeggios in the left hand which provide, as it were, so reassuring a support for the bare consecutive fifths which outline the melody above?

As if to mark his return to the classical fold, it will be noticed that Satie has here renounced the bar-less notation to which he had remained faithful for so many years as well as those humoristic admonitions to the performer which appear on all the piano works later than *Gymnopédies*—which also conform to the bar-line tradition. Thus the wheel has come full circle. The *Five Nocturnes* and the *Minuet* of 1920 (probably intended as the first of a set of three pieces) were the last works Satie was to write for the piano; and in them he achieved that fusion of form and content on a purely musical plane towards which the serious musician in his strangely composite make-up had consciously or unconsciously been striving for three decades.

Before leaving the piano works mention should be made of the solitary work which Satie wrote for piano and violin (in 1912) and to which he gave the fantastic title of *Choses vues à droite et à gauche (sans lunettes)*. As usual there are three pieces in the set: 'Choral hypocrite', 'Fugue à tatons', and 'Fantaisie musculaire'. The Choral is prefaced by these words: 'My chorals equal those of Bach with this difference: there are not so many of them, and they are less pretentious.' These pieces are also plentifully sprinkled with characteristic admonitions to the performers: e.g., 'with the hand on the conscience', 'from the top of the teeth', 'with tenderness and fatality', 'sheepishly and coldly', etc.; but their charm is undeniable, and they can be recommended to violinists on the look-out for something a little out of the ordinary.

Our survey of Satie's pianistic output is now completed. The lesson it teaches has been well summed up by M. Koechlin in the following terms: 'Satie, with extreme discretion and by means of discoveries which, though seemingly trivial, yet called for infinite imagination, observation, cunning and musicianship combined, depicts for us the grotesque in a style the artistic value of which we have not yet perhaps fully grasped.'

It remains for us now to see how this unique personality was able to express itself in other branches of his art.

Chapter VII

The Songs

As a song-writer Erik Satie was not lacking in originality. In all his vocal works, which are not numerous, he has his own way of treating the human voice. With a complete disregard for 'effect' one feels his chief concern is to render the meaning and spirit of the text rather than to write a 'melody'. In this respect he was closer to Debussy and Ravel than to Gounod or Massenet. His earliest known works were, as is the case with most young composers, in the form of songs, written while he was still a boy and published by his father. It is a pity that 'Les Anges', 'Les Fleurs' and 'Sylvie' have disappeared, though it is not difficult to imagine what they must have been like. After that, he wrote no more for the voice until 1914 when the curious *Trois Poèmes d'Amour* appeared: 'Ne suis que grain de sable', 'Suis chauve de naissance', and 'Ta parure est secrète'. The words, by himself, are humoristic in a sort of archaic way, but the melody is more like Plainsong. Indeed it has been pointed out[28] that the first song bears a striking, almost note-for-note resemblance to the Easter Liturgical Office 'Victimae paschali laudes'—additional evidence of the influence of Gregorian music on Satie's style, already apparent in the early *Ogives*, the *Gnossiennes*, the Four Preludes, the *Danses Gothiques* and the *Messe des Pauvres*. The parallel is indeed striking, and affords an interesting sidelight on the working of the composer's mind:

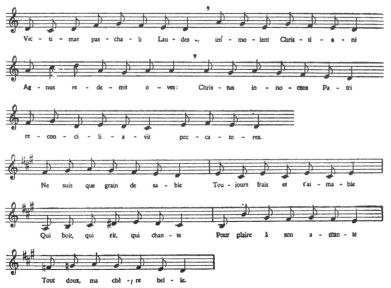

Two years later came the delightful set of *Trois Mélodies* ('La Statue de Bronze', 'Daphénéo', and 'Le Chapelier') which contain the essence of Satie the ironist, the wit, and the skilful parodist. The first (the words are by Léon-Paul Fargue) describes the ennui of the great metallic frog to be found in tea-gardens and such places into whose wide-open jaws people amuse themselves by throwing wooden balls, but who would much rather be with others of his kind in the pond 'blowing bubbles of music out of the moonlight's soap'.

In 'Daphénéo' (words by 'M. God'—Godebski) Chrysaline

[28] See *La Revue Musicale*, November 1936, pp. 334-5, article by Léon Guichard.

asks Daphénéo what tree it is whose fruit consists of birds that weep, and is told that the tree is a 'oisetier' (bird-tree). To this Chrysaline replies, 'très étonné', with a breathless 'Ah! . . . I thought, Daphénéo, that nut-trees (noisetiers) produced nuts'. 'Yes, Chrysaline, nut-trees produce nuts, but bird-trees produce birds that weep'. And the song ends with another 'Ah! . . .' from Chrysaline ('encore étonné'). The effect is irresistibly comic, although the means employed by Satie in turning this bit of nonsense into music are classic in their sobriety and restraint. The third song (dedicated to Igor Stravinsky) is a setting of words by René Chalupt 'after *Alice in Wonderland*', expressing the Mad Hatter's surprise that his watch is three days slow, although he is always careful to grease it with 'the best butter'; even plunging it into his tea does not put it right. Satie, with imperturbable gravity, marks his melody 'genre Gounod' and carries off the joke in a most polished style.

The *Quatre Petites Mélodies*, composed in 1920, belong unmistakably to their epoch. Less spontaneous, and also less characteristic of their author, these songs are settings of words by Lamartine, Jean Cocteau, Raymond Radiguet, and anonymous 18th century. The first, 'Elégie', is dedicated to the memory of Claude Debussy 'in memory of an admiring and tender friendship of thirty years'. Its somewhat awkward prosody is matched by harmonic angularities which, one feels, do not quite 'come off':

For bass clef in first bar read treble.

and the concluding bars are somewhat disconcerting. At all events it cannot be said that there is any attempt here to imitate Debussy's style.

The setting of Cocteau's 'Danseuse' is suitably angular; the 18th century drinking song is treated amusingly; and Radiguet's ironic little 'Adieu' ('Amiral, ne crois pas déchoir En agitant ton vieux mouchoir, C'est la coutume de chasser ainsi les mouches du passé') is carried on a waltz-rhythm slightly distorted in the manner of the 'twenties.

With the *Ludions*, however, the last of Satie's purely vocal works, written two years before he died, on texts by Léon-Paul Fargue, we are on familiar ground again. The old Satiean wit and fantasy are once more in evidence—and these nonsense verses are treated either in a 'popular' music-hall style, or else with a mock seriousness, as in 'Air du Poète', that matches the deliberately ludicrous words. Satie is here at his most Parisian; he has adjusted his pince-nez at an ironic angle and become the intellectual enjoying a literary joke in company with an author who is perhaps his nearest counterpart in literature. The result, in *Ludions*, of this Satie-cum-Fargue collaboration is irresistible.

The last and most important of the vocal works is, of course, —*Socrate, Drame symphonique en trois parties avec voix* composed in 1918. It belongs to the period of what is usually referred to as 'musique d'ameublement' of which some account has already been given; and if by this is meant a form of art which unfolds itself calmly and untouched by emotions, relying on an internal equilibrium rather than on violent contrasts of mood and style, then *Socrate* may be said to conform to this definition.

But *Socrate* is something more than this; it is anything but soulless, and is indeed rich in poetic content and imaginative vision. The circumstances under which it was composed and dedicated to the Princesse de Polignac have already been described; it only remains now to examine it in greater detail.

The work is scored for four sopranos and an orchestra consisting of single wood-wind, including a cor anglais, 1 horn, 1 trumpet, harp, kettle-drums and strings. The original score has never been published, only the instrumental parts. The MS copy I have seen, which is I believe the only one extant, does not appear to be in Satie's handwriting. The three parts into which *Socrate* is divided are, as regards the text (the translation is that of Victor Cousin) taken from the *Symposium*, *Phaedrus* and *Phaedo* respectively—three of the most famous of Plato's *Dialogues*.

The first ('Portrait of Socrates') is a dialogue between Socrates and Alcibiades; the second ('By the banks of the Ilyssus') is a dialogue between Socrates and Phaedrus; the third (the 'Death of Socrates') is a narration for a single voice (Phaedo). One can understand the apprehension Satie felt at the prospect of setting such a text to music. Above all he was aware of the danger of 'adding to' the beauty of Plato's text—hence the extraordinary self-effacement and detachment of the music which very rarely attempts to underline or enhance the emotional significance of the words. With characteristic modesty Satie contented himself with supplying, as it were, a musical background in the orchestra against which the voices of the narrators are made to rise and fall in a kind of supple *mélopée* closely modelled on the inflections of natural speech. He did not ask for any vocal 'effects'; indeed it is clear that what he had in mind was a reading rather than a singing voice since he took care to mark the vocal part from the beginning as a 'Récit' (narration) adding the words 'en lisant', (as if reading). The instrumental accompaniment seems strangely independent of what is being sung, and consists mainly of recurring patterns based on bare harmonies in which sevenths, fourths and fifths are predominant,[29] but the texture is throughout so limpid and transparent that the words, if properly delivered, can be heard as if outlined in light. The pastoral character of the second section ('By the banks of the Ilyssus'—in flowing 6/8 time) is admirably suggested in the cool harmonies and easy lilt of the vocal line:

[29]The following is a typical accompanying figure:

97

But it is in the final scene in which Phaedo describes the death of Socrates that the music attains a poignancy which might seem incredible in view of the simplicity of the means employed. A grave note is struck in the very first bars in an ascending sequence of triads which recurs at intervals suggesting the tolling of a bell. But there is never the slightest over-emphasis, no attempt at dramatisation, no overloading of the emotional content; the beautiful and pathetic narration is allowed to move unhurriedly to its climax discreetly supported and sustained by a musical figuration which is a miracle of reticence and sobriety. And yet there are passages of sheer musical beauty, as for example this where Socrates takes the cup of hemlock and drinks it 'avec une tranquillité et une douceur merveilleuse':

Socra . te porta la coupe à ses lè . vres   et la but a.vec u.ne tran.

quil.li.té   et u.ne dou.ceur   merveilleu . se.

Almost the only touch of dramatic realism in the music occurs at the passage describing how the poison has begun to work; the stiffening and chilling of the body of Socrates is expressed in a harsh discord, C sharp against C natural; but the music flows imperturbably on, with no rhythmic disturbance to the end. After the famous 'Crito, we owe a cock to Aesculapius; do not forget to settle that debt', death is ushered in by a steady pulsing chord of E and A over a pedal A, four crotchets to a bar, with a heavy toll-like accent on the first beat, repeated forty-four times producing an indescribable effect of bleakness and desolation. The voice part is also confined to the two notes—A and E. At the forty-fifth bar, the chord is shifted up a tone, with the most poignant effect, and reiterated 16 times in the key of B. Then for two bars it drops again to A (always without the third) and after the last spoken words, the orchestra has a two-bar cadence like a sigh closing on an indeterminate 6/4 chord, F sharp, B, F sharp. It is as if with the departure of the soul of Socrates a great emptiness had descended on the earth; and the music dies away, exhausted in spirit and drained of its life's blood.

Thus ends one of the strangest works in the annals of music. Both in conception and in execution it is literally unique; neither before nor since has anything similar ever been attempted. That critics and the public under-estimated and misunderstood it thirty years ago is not surprising; Erik Satie was once again ahead of his times. Today one can only feel sorry for the public that hissed and tittered at the first performance, still more so for critics like Jean Marnold of the *Mercure de France* who imagined he saw in *Socrate* endless reminiscences of *Boris* and *Pelléas* (sic) and dismissed the work contemptuously as 'non-existent'. Even present-day audiences may find it difficult and disconcerting; for the truth is *Socrate* moves on an aesthetic plane so detached and remote from normal experience that it does demand from the listener a concentrated effort and a willingness to divest himself of preconceived notions about music before he can enter into the necessary state of receptivity. This may not be 'great' music; I would not make that claim; but it is music so singular and of such peculiar potency in its own rather ghostly way that it seems, as it were, to be outside time and period, and so 'dateless' that if it survives at all it will probably seem no more and no less 'contemporary' two hundred years hence than it seems to us today.

Chapter VIII

The Stage Works; ballets

SATIE WAS 26 YEARS old when he composed his first ballet *Uspud* on a scenario by his friend J. P. Contamine de Latour. It has already been related how he offered it to the Director of the Paris Opéra and with what results. . . .

As the work is something of a curiosity and throws an interesting light on Satie's mentality at that time I have thought it worth while to transcribe from an extremely rare printed cópy —probably the only one extant—of the scenario of this extraordinary work. See Appendix B.

One of the minor peculiarities of this brochure, which was issued by the joint authors after the rejection of their work by the Director of the Opéra, but nevertheless inscribed 'présenté' (offered)—not 're-présenté', which would have meant performed—'au théâtre national de l'opéra le 20 dec. 1892', is that the text is printed without any capital letters. This little typographic eccentricity was something of a novelty in the eighteen-nineties, although today it has been adopted by the more esoteric literary reviews as well as by 'la haute couture'. Nothing survives of the music except the few bars printed in this booklet of which a facsimile appears in the illustration facing this page.

The synopsis of this extraordinary creation is as follows. Upsud, dressed as a Persian, appears on a deserted beach. In the centre there is a statue, in the distance the sea. In the Second Act Uspud is converted, after having resisted the assault of demons disguised as animals of divers kinds, such as— dogs, jackals, tortoises, goats, fish, lynx, tiger-wolfs, oxen, sea-woodcocks, unicorns, sheep, antelope, ants, spiders, gnus, serpents, blue 'agouti-boucs', baboons, 'cuculu', crabs, albatross, 'pacre', ostriches, moles, secretary-birds, old bulls, red caterpillars, 'bouti', 'pogos', boars, crocodiles, bison, etc., etc.

The Third Act is an Apotheosis: Uspud, torn to pieces by demons, is raised up to Christ through the intervention of the Christian Church.

With the exception of the Rose+Croix musics, already dealt with, Satie wrote no more for the theatre until 1899 when he produced two of his most charming and characteristic works. These were the miniature opera for marionettes, *Geneviève de Brabant* (libretto by Contamine de Latour) and *Jack in the Box* written for a pantomime by his friend Depaquit and destined for the Comédie Parisienne. The MSS of both these works were discovered after the composer's death behind one of the pianos in his room at Arcueil. Both are now published in the Universal Edition, *Jack in the Box* having been orchestrated by Darius Milhaud and produced as a ballet by the Diaghilev Company, with *décors* by Derain, in 1926.

Another early stage work was the comic operetta *Pousse*

heureux melou l'estropié; saint vequin l'écorché; sainte purine la déchaussée; saint plau moine prêcheur; sainte benu avec une hache. leurs voix appellent uspud au martyre.

une soif inextinguible de souffrance le pénètre. il déchire sa robe de bure et apparaît vêtu de la tunique blanche des néophytes. il se remet en prière

une légion de démons surgit de tous les côtés. ils revêtent des formes montrueuses: chiens noirs avec une corne d'or sur le front; corps de poissons avec des têtes et des ailes d'oiseaux; géants au chef de taureau, soufflant du feu par les narines.

uspud recommande son esprit au seigneur, puis se livre aux démons qui le déchirent avec fureur.

l'église chrétienne apparait, éblouissante de clarté et escortée de deux anges, portant des palmes et des couronnes. elle prend l'âme d'uspud dans ses bras et l'enlève vers le christ; qui rayonne dans le ciel.

Reproduced by kind permission of M. Roland-Manuel

Portrait of Satie as a young man
by Suzanne Valadon

l'Armour by Maurice de Féraudy, for which Satie composed in 1905 a few 'numbers' which have disappeared. It seems that this operetta was produced at Monte Carlo in 1913 under the title of *Coco Chéri* . . .

1913—this was the year in which Satie, who was now becoming famous as a musical humorist, through the medium of his pieces for the piano, conceived and brought forth a work for the stage in which he was his own librettist—*Le piège de Méduse* —*comédie en un acte de M. Erik Satie (avec musique du même Monsieur)*. Considered as a prelude to *Parade*, *Mercure*, and *Relâche*, *Le Piège* is the first of Satie's definitely 'avant-garde' works. Indeed it anticipated Dada, though it was to some extent a product of the same spirit that was animating the early surrealist painters who were then coming to the fore, even though they had not yet received the Surrealist label (e.g., Chagall and Chirico).

This, no doubt, was one of the reasons why *Le Piège* had to wait until 1921 before being staged. Once again Satie was a move ahead.

Le Piège de Méduse is scored for clarinet, trumpet, trombone, violin, 'cello, double-bass and percussion. It has four personages: the Baron Méduse, his 'fille-de-lait' (!) Frisette; her lover Astolfo; and the Baron's valet Polycarpe. There is also a stuffed monkey, Jonas, who executes dances between the scenes. The Baron has eye-trouble and is tormented by his valet who is extremely insolent and *tutoie*'s him all the time. The Baron tries to trap Astolfo by asking him a preposterous question about dancing with his eyes; as he gives a satisfactory answer, he will be allowed to marry Frisette. The following is a specimen of the dialogue (from an original MS in Satie's handwriting):

Scene I

Baron Méduse:	My steward will finish this job. My eyes are too bad. My sight is going.
Polycarpe:	Monsieur le Baron rang?
Méduse:	My sight is going.
Polycarpe:	I say! I've got to go out tonight; I absolutely must —do you hear?
Méduse:	Tonight?
Polycarpe:	Yes, tonight—I must.
Méduse:	Where are you going?
Polycarpe:	I'm going to a billiard match. What a match! Napoleon will be there. I mean, of course, the Napoleon of billiards—the real one.

Méduse:	You can put off this match of yours till tomorrow.
Polycarpe:	You're mad! Put off a billiard match! Whoever heard of such a thing!—if only Napoleon could hear you . . . . (*goes out gesticulating*).

End of Scene I.

Méduse:	I don't recognise the horse's voice. No—I give it up.
Polycarpe:	(*Bringing a card on a tray*)— Don't receive him; he'll only make me late. It begins punctually over there. What a splendid match! You ought to come, you know. But you're too proud to go out with me—a humble working-man, a trade unionist . . . .

(Dance of the Monkey).

PARADE

'*Ballet réaliste en un tableau. Thème de Jean Cocteau; Rideau, Décors et Costumes de Pablo Picasso; Chorégraphie de Léonide Massine.*' *First performed at the Théâtre du Chatelet, Paris, on May 18th, 1917 by Serge de Diaghilev's Russian Ballet (with Massine Lopokova and Woizikovski); Conductor: Ernest Ansermet.*

With the arrival of Diaghilev and his Russian Ballet on the European scene in the years immediately preceding the First World War, it was inevitable that sooner or later Satie would find himself involved in this epoch-making enterprise which was gradually absorbing all the best talent in Europe.

Cocteau has related[30] how the first idea for *Parade* came to him during a period of leave from the front in April 1915 (he was then in the Army) after hearing Satie and Ricardo Viñes play the *Morceaux en forme de Poire* for piano duet. 'A kind of telepathy inspired us simultaneously with a desire to collaborate. A week later I returned to the front leaving Satie with a bundle of notes and sketches which were to provide him with the theme of the Chinaman, the little American Girl, and the Acrobat (there was then only one acrobat).'

The score of *Parade* is remarkable for its almost mechanical, clockwork-like precision and its completely unemotional objectivity. It opens with a Choral (omitted in the piano 4-hand arrangement) which leads into the 'Prelude of the Red Curtain' —a short fugal exposition which is followed, as the curtain rises, by the entry of the first Manager.

[30] In *Coq et l'Arlequin*, 1918.

This 'Managers' theme' is one of Satie's most original and remarkable inventions, so admirably evocative of the bustle and
monotonous, insect-like activity of the fair-ground. Next comes
the Scene of the Chinese Conjuror who juggles with an egg, spits
fire, burns himself and stamps to put out the sparks, etc. . . .
while serene fragments of soothing melody are heard in the
orchestra over an insistent *ostinato* bass. The first Manager then
executes a silent dance without music and is followed by the
'Little American Girl' who 'mounts a race-horse, rides a bicycle,
quivers like pictures on the films, imitates Charlie Chaplin,
chases a thief with a revolver, boxes, dances a Ragtime, goes to
sleep, is shipwrecked, rolls on the grass on an April morning,
buys a Kodak, etc., etc.' The music now becomes syncopated in
the manner fashionable at the time (notably in the 'Ragtime du
Paquebot', marked 'Triste' in the score) until the Acrobats enter
to a sort of music-hall waltz tune with cunningly displaced

103

accents and monotonously repeated phrases bandied about in the orchestra like the balls which jugglers keep going in the air simultaneously. Cocteau says of the Acrobats: 'We tried to invest them with the melancholy of a Sunday evening after the circus when the sounding of "Lights Out" obliges the children to put on their overcoats again, while casting a last glance at the ring.'

The ballet ends with a frenzied dance of the Managers who finally collapse while the Chinaman, the acrobats and the Girl leave the empty theatre and explain in their turn to the audience, as the Managers have all along been trying to do, that the real show takes place inside; what they have seen is only the 'Parade'.

The final dance of the Managers, under their heavy wooden 'carcasses', is accompanied by an orchestral *tutti* thundering out the theme which introduced them at the beginning; and the ballet is rounded off by a continuation of the opening fugue ('Suite au Prélude du Rideau Rouge') culminating in an impressive cadence and a final close in C major.

Whatever else it may be *Parade* is a landmark in the history of the theatre; it was revolutionary in every detail—scenery, costumes, choreography and music. Naturally the critics to a large extent missed the point. That they should have thought Satie's orchestra poor because it was lacking in impressionist sauce is perhaps comprehensible; that they should have thought it a mere 'din' can only be explained, as Cocteau points out, 'by the phenomenon of suggestion—The word "cubism" wrongly introduced, *suggested* an orchestra to them. Otherwise the absolute simplicity of the score renders their indignation inexplicable. . . .'

And he goes on to give the following résumé which explains the whole aesthetic upon which this ballet is based—a ballet which, although imperfectly realised owing to material circumstances, remains, to quote his own words, 'an open window through which may be had a glimpse of what the modern theatre ought to be'.

'The arrangement of *Parade* for four hands', he writes, 'is from beginning to end an architectural masterpiece; that is what ears accustomed to vagueness and thrills are unable to understand. A fugue comes bustling along and gives birth to the actual melancholy rhythm of the fair. Then come the three dances. Their numerous themes, each distinct from the other, like separate objects, succeed one another without being developed, and do not get entangled. A metronomical unity governs each of these enumerations which are superimposed upon the simple outlines of each character and upon the imaginative ideas evoked by them. The Chinaman, the little American Girl and the Acrobats represent varieties of "nostalgia" hitherto unknown, so great is the degree of verisimilitude with which they are expressed. No humbug, no repetition, no underhand caresses, no feverishness or miasma; Satie never "stirs up the mud". His is the poetical imagination of childhood moulded by a master technician.'

It is surprising that *Parade* has been comparatively seldom performed. Diaghilev, questioned about this, is reported to have replied: 'It is one of the best bottles in my cellar; I do not want to have it shaken up too often . . .' Nevertheless there would surely be a place for it in the repertory of some contemporary ballet company who would be prepared to face the difficulties of production; provided the Picasso sets and costumes were still available. Of all the stage works of Satie *Parade* is the one which would have the best chance of success today—whether or not it were given with all the somewhat eccentric instrumentation originally planned but never fully realised (revolvers, sirens, clappers, typewriters, lottery-wheels, Morse apparatus, etc.). These could be dispensed with, but the essence of the music would remain—music which caused Stravinsky, after the première of *Parade*, to bracket Satie with Bizet and Chabrier.

MERCURE

'*Poses plastiques en trois tableaux*'. First performance '*La Cigale*' Paris, June 15th, 1924, *scenery and costumes by Picasso; choreography by Massine.*

Mercure has been called a painter's ballet, and indeed the part played by Picasso who designed the costumes and the sets is at least as important as the music. Many of Satie's former admirers were disappointed with his score, and on the first night the Surrealists manifested violently in favour of Picasso, creating such a hubbub in the theatre that the curtain had to be lowered in the middle of the performance. Afterwards the Surrealist group issued a 'Declaration' entitled *Hommage à Picasso* in the following terms: 'We hereby place on record our profound and whole-hearted admiration for Picasso who, scorning what is sanctioned by tradition, has never ceased to foster present-day neuroses and to express them in masterly fashion. And now, in *Mercure*, in the full exercise of his audacious genius, he has been

105

met once again with complete incomprehension. In the light of this event, which is highly significant, Picasso, *far more than any of those associated with him*, appears today as the eternal personification of youth and the undisputed master of the situation'. This was signed, among others, by the writers Aragon, Breton and Soupault, the painter Max Ernst, and Francis Poulenc. Nevertheless, Satie's music cannot be dismissed as entirely devoid of interest. There are twelve principal scenes: 'Night', 'Dance of Tenderness', 'Signs of the Zodiac', 'Mercury's Dance', 'Dance of the Graces', 'Bath of the Graces', 'Flight of Mercury', 'Anger of Cerberus', 'Letter Polka', 'New Dance', 'Chaos', 'Finale'. As already stated Satie gave his score intentionally a 'popular' character, with a fair-ground atmosphere; and there is no doubt that the association of this clear-cut almost naïve music with the highly sophisticated and ingenious scenic constructions of Picasso produced an impression of incongruity, which some people found too disconcerting. The whole case is an interesting one from a psychological point of view, as it shows how little inclined Satie was to make any concessions in any direction; his work had always to conform to whatever ideas or theories he had in mind at any given moment, regardless of circumstances. Nowhere is what Constant Lambert has called 'the static abstraction of Satie's best work'[31] more in evidence than in *Mercure*; as an example of the composer's strict avoidance of anything approaching direct 'illustration' the same writer instances his original treatment of the theme of 'Chaos' in this Ballet which is suggested by 'a skilful blending of two previously heard movements, one the suave and sustained "Nouvelle Danse", the other the robust and snappy "Polka des Lettres". These two tunes are so disparate in mood that the effect, mentally speaking, is one of complete chaos; yet it is achieved by strictly musical and even academic means which consolidate the formal cohesion of the ballet as a whole'.

RELÂCHE

'*Ballet instantanéiste en deux actes; un entr'acte cinématographique, et "la queue du chien". Scénario et décors de Francis Picabia. Cinématographie de René Clair*'. First performed by Jean Borlin's Swedish Ballet at the Théâtre des Champs-Élysées, Paris, November 29th, 1924.

This was Satie's last work; he died the following year. The story of how *Relâche* came to be written and the scandal it

[31]*Music Ho!* p. 90.

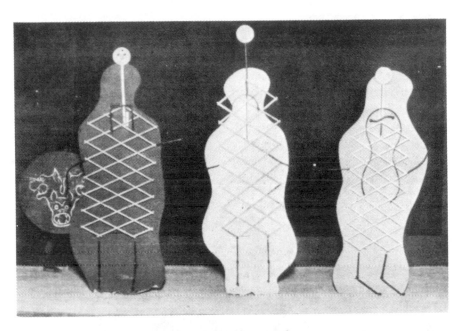

Picasso's designs for *Mercure*

Frontispiece to *Relâche*

caused has already been related; here are some details about its
content and construction. The score bears the following in-
scription signed by Picabia:

Relâche, like Infinity, has no friends. In order to have friends one
has to be very ill, so ill that one can no longer keep them away.

If Satie ever liked *Relâche*, no doubt he liked it in the same way
that he liked Kirsch or roast mutton, or his umbrella!

Relâche, has no meaning; it is the pollen of our epoch. A speck of
dust on our fingertips and the drawing fades away. . . . We must
think about it at a distance, not try to touch it. . . .

And on the frontispiece appears the motto:·

When will one lose the habit of explaining everything. . . .

Certainly it would be difficult to 'explain' *Relâche*. Such
action as there is is completely arbitrary; the characters are a
Man and a Woman, and a male *corps de ballet*. There is a dance
with a wheelbarrow, a dance with a crown, a dance with a
revolving door; the men dress and undress on the stage, etc.,
etc., and all this takes place against a background of giant gramo-
phone discs piled on the top of each other so as to present their
flat surfaces to the audience and forming a solid wall towering
to the height of the proscenium. In short a 'spectacle Dada', intentionally grotesque and devoid of meaning. And for this crazy
scenario Satie solemnly sat down and produced a succession of
serious and rather dry dance-movements—*entrées* and *rentrées*,
with here and there a popular tune austerely disguised or
blatantly proclaimed so as to give the public something they
could recognise. In this passage from the scene of the 'Men
Undressing' he introduces, for example, a fragment, disguised,
of 'Cadet Roussel':

enchaîner

The authors of *Relâche* aimed at being 'anti-academic'; the
critics merely thought they were being rather vulgar. Satie especially had a bad press; one critic wrote that he had 'achieved

without much effort a perfect replica of the lowest of low cabaret music'. This, of course, is quite untrue; whatever its shortcomings this music is not lacking in style and technical accomplishment. Darius Milhaud, on the other hand, speaks of the high degree of 'authenticity and perfection' revealed in Satie's music to *Relâche*; but this of course applies to everything he wrote. No matter what genre he attempted he never failed to produce something that fitted that genre completely. There is never any feeling of ambiguity—still less of 'fake' or insincerity—in the whole range of his production, from the music-hall songs written for Paulette Darty to the grave austerity of *Socrate*. And this quality of 'authenticity' is something quite distinct from the actual intrinsic value of the music, which is obviously a very variable factor. And so we can agree with Milhaud's remark concerning *Relâche*, and at the same time express the opinion that considered from a purely musical standpoint this ballet is one of the least interesting of Satie's works. It reveals no new aspect of his art, and the music, unlike that of *Parade*, for example, seems only to have a shadowy existence when divorced from its theatrical setting. An exception must be made, however, for the film music of the *Entr'acte Cinématographique*, which has already been discussed in a previous chapter.

In some ways it would have perhaps been more fitting had *Socrate* been Satie's swan-song, or even the piano *Nocturnes*, because it is in these works that his peculiar and unique genius seems to have come to its final fruition. But the comedian in him had to have one last fling, and so the last glimpse we catch of the 'Bon Maître d'Arcueil' is in *Relâche*, making a rather wry grimace.

Among the stage-works that were contemplated but never completed were a ballet, *La Naissance de Vénus*, for which Derain was to have designed the décor, and an opera, *Paul et Virginie*, libretto by Cocteau and Raymond Radiguet. Although the latter was a good deal talked about at one time, there is no evidence that Satie ever started on its composition, and no trace of a score was found after his death.

Part Three: The Man

Chapter IX

His Writings

THE FOREGOING PAGES, I hope, may have succeeded in giving the reader who has hitherto had no opportunity of acquainting himself at first-hand with Satie's music some idea of its variety and outstanding characteristics. Such a reader may feel himself attracted or repelled, as the case may be, but whatever his reaction may be he will be compelled to admit that the question of the composer's personality has loomed very large and influenced him in his judgement to a considerable extent.

And here we touch upon a crucial aspect of the 'cas Satie'— the question of whether it is the man or his music that has contributed most to the creation of the Satie 'legend'. With the majority of composers this question does not usually arise; it is their music that counts for us and nothing else; only rarely do we take the trouble to get acquainted with the man behind the music and learn about his life and character. But in the case of Erik Satie the two are so inextricably mixed up together that it is impossible to separate one from the other. The reason for this is, I think, partly that whereas most composers express themselves in an accepted and more or less familiar idiom, Satie practically invented a mode of expression which belongs to him and to him alone. And the only key to this private language is the character of the artist who invented it. Consequently in order to understand Satie's music it is essential to know what sort of a man he was. How did it happen that the rather eccentric son of a Scotswoman and a bourgeois French provincial grew up to be a sort of *éminence grise* behind the throne of twentieth-century French music? The story is one of the strangest in the

109

annals of any art—just as the place that Satie occupies in musical history is unique.

For we cannot, I think, escape the conclusion that from a historical and documentary point of view Satie the man is, in the last resort, more important than Satie the musician. In other words, his true significance is to be sought in his 'teachings', in his personality, and in his whole attitude towards, and ideas about music, rather than in what he actually achieved as a composer. Or, as M. Roland-Manuel has put it: 'The importance of Satie lies not so much in what he did as in what he caused to be done'. Let us see then if we can discover what he accomplished in this way, and by what means. To do this we shall have to take into account not only the musical theorist, but the whole complex personality of the man: hermit, saint, philosopher, wit, buffoon, Socratic ironist, enemy of convention, champion of youth, pioneer and fearless explorer along new and untried paths in art.

Let us, to begin with, examine a self-portrait, showing us the artist as seen by himself. It was written by Satie for a publisher's catalogue,[32] and reads as follows:

M. Erik Satie was born at Honfleur (Calvados) on May 17, 1866. He is considered to be the strangest musician of our time. He classes himself among the 'fantasists' who are, in his opinion, 'highly respectable people'. He often says to his friends: 'Although born shortsighted I am long-sighted by inclination. . . . Shun pride: of all the evils from which we suffer this is the most constipating. Let those unhappy people whose sight does not see me (sic) blacken their tongues and burst their ears'.

Such is the every-day conversation of M. Erik Satie. We must not forget that the Master is looked upon by very many of the 'younger' school as the forerunner and apostle of the revolution now taking place in music; MM. Maurice Ravel, E. Vuillermoz, Robert Brussel, M.-D. Calvocoressi, J. Ecorcheville, Roland-Manuel, etc., have introduced him as such, and their affirmation is based on facts the accuracy of which is undisputed.

After having essayed the loftiest genres the eminent composer now presents some of his humoristic works. This is what he says about his humour: 'My humour resembles that of Cromwell. I also owe much to Christopher Columbus, because the American spirit has occasionally tapped me on the shoulder and I have been delighted to feel its ironically glacial bite.'

We would mention here the *Véritables Préludes Flasques (pour un chien)* of which the great pianist Ricardo Viñes gave such an outstanding performance at the Salle Pleyel (Société Nationale) on

[32]Kindly communicated by M. Roland-Manuel, owner of the very rare original.

His Writings

April 5, 1913; the *Descriptions Automatiques*, which had a considerable success at the Conservatoire concert of the Société Musicale Indépendante on June 5, 1913, and which the same Ricardo Viñes played with an atmosphere of secrecy that was irresistibly droll.

This is what the Master has to say about these pieces: 'I wrote the *Descriptions Automatiques* for my birthday. This work is a pendant to the *Véritables Préludes Flasques*. It is clear that the Deflated, the Insignificant and the Puffed-Up Ones will not appreciate these works. Let them swallow their beards! Let them dance on their own stomachs!'

To the above-mentioned works must be added the amusing *Embryons Desséchés*, the joyful *Croquis et Agaceries d'un Gros Bonhomme en Bois*. The *Chapitres Tournés en Tous Sens*, and the *Vieux Séquins et Vieilles Cuirasses* will come next and complete this curious and pleasingly original series.

The beautiful and limpid *Aperçus Désagréables* (piano four hands)—Pastorale, Choral and Fugue—are written in the most superior style and enable us to understand why the subtle composer is justified in declaring: 'Before writing a work I go round it several times accompanied by myself.'

This curious document, with its deliberate exaggerations and somewhat aggressive facetiousness, must be unique in the literature of publishers' 'blurbs'. And how its author must have enjoyed writing it. For it all helped to build up the atmosphere of mystery with which he loved to surround himself.

Behind that screen he could live and work unmolested. For he had need of a protective disguise, being in reality the most timid of men, as those who knew him intimately have testified. And as sometimes happens with shy people his timidity was apt to turn to truculence. He preferred to attack rather than endure attack; sensitive to criticism, he would carry the war into the enemy's country and anticipate the onslaught that he feared. His susceptibility was such as to render all personal relationship with him extremely difficult and hazardous; sooner or later he quarrelled with all his friends, often on the most absurd pretexts, imagining an insult or a slight where none had been intended. With a friend who accidentally damaged one of his beloved umbrellas he ceased from that moment to be on speaking terms; another friend he never forgave for having inadvertently taken his piece of bread at table. Such trivial incidents as these assumed gigantic proportions in Satie's imagination; he saw in them a sinister desire to insult or humiliate him. And his anger, when roused, could be terrific. Baseness of any kind, real or imagined, he could not tolerate. For him there was no middle

111

way; he was incapable of compromise. Did he not declare, not long before his death, 'Il faut être intransigeant jusqu'au bout'? It was the only possible attitude for him—even though it brought him enemies. And all his life he encountered opposition, incomprehension and suspicion. Few musicians can ever have been so persistently persecuted and derided. But in his solitude and voluntary isolation he was strong enough to defy or ignore persecution and derision; his convictions gave him that strength, and the faith that was in him—faith in the art which he loved and served according to his lights.

Satie was not a 'primitive' like the 'Douanier' Rousseau with whom he has sometimes been compared. It is true that much of the charm of his music lies in its spontaneity and freshness; but his art was not entirely instinctive as was the case with Rousseau. No doubt, considered purely as an artist, Rousseau rose to greater heights in his creative work than Satie ever did, by virtue of some mysterious 'divine efflatus' or dæmon by whom his brush was guided; how else can one account for the emergence of the purest masterpieces from a brain which in other respects might well have belonged to the merest simpleton?

Satie, on the other hand, possessed one of the shrewdest and most critical intellects of his time. In congenial company he was capable of conversing on a wide range of topics outside his own particular province, and at one time as a young man he had been a voracious reader, spending hours at the Bibliothèque Nationale studying such subjects as Gothic art, medieval illuminated manuscripts and liturgy. He had an excellent memory which enabled him to retain throughout his life a considerable body of knowledge of a heterogeneous kind, with fragments of which his conversation was liable at any time to be unexpectedly seasoned. His political opinions (if any) were left-wing (was he not a member of the 'Soviet d'Arcueil'?); he loved children and animals; he accepted poverty with philosophical humility, but if money came his way he would enjoy spending it and was extremely generous. Of its true value he was as ignorant as a child. He had no conception of the meaning of wealth—and certainly no desire to possess it. It was against his principles to borrow; but he would accept and even solicit small gifts of money from his friends without hesitation. Whereas a loan would have seemed to him a sordid financial transaction, the acceptance of a gift did not offend his pride. Knowing nothing of 'big money' and caring less he was content all his life to sell his music to his publishers for purely nominal sums. That was the

plane on which he lived—one of almost complete detachment
from all those cares and petty worries which make most people's,
even most artists', lives a burden. He cultivated solitude, both
physical and spiritual; as Darius Milhaud observes: 'He preferred to be alone with himself the better to keep faith with the
ideas which were essential to the defence of his work'.

At the same time, provided we are convinced of the essential
gravity and significance of Satie the composer, it would be un-
pardonable if we failed to discern in Satie the man a wit of the
first order, a profound observer and critic of mankind, and one
of the most authentic and entertaining 'eccentrics' who have
ever enlivened with their presence the drabness of our human
scene. How well Satie sensed his own essential loneliness in his
self-appointed double role, first as a creator who looked at the
world through the candid eyes of a child (pungently expressed
in one of his most famous *mots:* 'Je suis venu au monde très jeune
dans un temps très vieux') and secondly as a cynic with a profound mistrust for his fellow-men and their so-called wisdom or
'experience' ('Quand j'étais jeune on me disait: Vous verrez
quand vous aurez cinquante ans. J'ai cinquante ans; je n'ai rien
vu'). Perhaps if the truth were known, so far from having seen
nothing, he saw too much—and too clearly. For he had the
clairvoyance of a child, which enabled him in Cocteau's words
'to teach what in our age is the greatest audacity—simplicity'.
He had in him something of a saint, something of a seer, and
something of a sorcerer. His attitude to life was, as we have seen,
Socratic; he questioned everything, took nothing at its accepted
value, and scoffed at whatever he thought was sham. But it was
his delight in and cultivation of what we may call the Art of Pure
Nonsense that gives him his unique position in the world of
music. For composers are not generally remarkable for their
sense of humour, and few of those who have possessed a modi-
cum have dared to allow its intrusion into their art. Mozart was
not above committing his 'musikalisches Spass', and Haydn
liked a little joke from time to time; but apart from stage works,
where such things are tolerated because of the requirements of
the text, there are not many examples of absolute music being
made a vehicle for humour.

A good many examples of Satie's particular brand have already
been given in the course of this work; but we have not yet
examined in any detail his purely literary output. This was
considerable, and during the last ten or fifteen years of his life
Satie was a fairly regular contributor to a number of periodicals

and reviews which however have long since disappeared from circulation. In many of these articles we can discern behind the jesting façade a shrewd and penetrating intellect and a critical faculty of no mean order. Almost invariably the tone is ironic, and no opportunity is lost of attacking officialdom, academicism, conventionality in all its forms—and especially music critics, a favourite target for Satie's barbed and bitter sarcasm. (His pet bugbears at the time were Jean Marnold of the *Mercure de France*, Emile Vuillermoz, and 'Willy').

The following extracts from an article entitled 'In Praise of Critics'[33] are in Satie's best and wittiest vein:

Last year I gave several lectures on 'Intelligence and the Appreciation of Music among Animals'[34]. Today I am going to speak to you about 'Intelligence and the Appreciation of Music among critics'. The subject is very similar . . . . We do not know enough about critics; we don't know what they have done or what they are capable of doing. In a word, they are as little understood as the animals although, like these, they have their uses. . . . Indeed, it was a critic who posed for Rodin's 'Penseur'. I learned this from another critic a fortnight ago—or maybe three weeks. This gave me a great deal of pleasure. Rodin had a weakness for critics . . . their advice was dear to him . . . very dear, too dear, altogether excessive. . . . There are three kinds of critics; the important ones, the less important ones, and the unimportant ones. The last two kinds do not exist; all critics are important. . . .

Physically, the critic is of a serious cast of countenance. He reminds one of a double-bassoon. He is himself a centre—a centre of gravity. . . .

There is no such thing as mediocrity or incompetence among critics. A critic who was mediocre or incompetent would be the laughing-stock of his fellow-critics, and it would be impossible for him to exercise his profession—I mean his priestly calling . . . and his life would be nothing but a long and terribly monotonous agony. . . . An artist can be imitated; a critic is inimitable . . . and exceedingly funny. How could one imitate a critic? I wonder . . . Anyway, what would be the point of trying? None at all. We have got the ORIGINAL—that is quite enough. . . . The brain of a critic is like a big department-store. It contains everything—orthopædy, science, bedding, the arts, travelling-rugs, a wide range of furnishings, letter-paper, both French and foreign, articles for smokers, gloves, umbrellas, woollen materials, hats, everything for sport, walking-sticks, optical instruments, perfumery, etc. The critic knows everything, sees everything, hears everything, touches everything, moves every-thing, eats everything, mixes everything up—and still goes on think-

[33]*Action*, August 1921. No. 8. Paris. See Appendix C.2.
[34]See pp. 120-121.

ing. What a man! . . . All our articles are guaranteed! During the hot weather the goods are kept inside—*INSIDE THE CRITIC*! . . . The critic is also a look-out man; one might add, a buoy. He marks the reefs which surround the coasts of the Human Mind. Near these coasts the critic keeps guard, magnificent in his clairvoyance from afar; he looks rather like a boundary-stone, but an intelligent and sympathetic one. . . . One can't sufficiently admire the courage of the first critic who ever appeared in the world. The rude inhabitants dwelling in the Ancient Night of Time no doubt received him with a kick in the pants, not realising that he was a forerunner to be revered. . . . He was certainly a Hero, in his own way. . . . The second, third, fourth and fifth critics certainly met with no better treatment . . . but helped to create a precedent. The Art of Criticism gave birth to itself. That was its first New Year's Day. . . . Long afterwards the Benefactors of Humanity learnt to organise themselves better. They founded Critics' Syndicates in all the great capitals, and in this way became persons of great importance—which proves that virtue is its own reward. Immediately the artists were put in fetters and treated like wildcats. It is only Right that Artists should be guided by the critics . . . they would do well to be more respectful to them, to listen to them attentively, to love them even, and to invite them often to the family table where they can sit between Uncle and Grandpapa. Let them follow my example—my good example. I am dazzled by the presence of a critic—he shines so brightly that I am forced to blink for an hour or more at a time. I kiss the ground his slippers have trodden—I drink his words in a long-stemmed wine-glass, simply from politeness.

I have made a special study of the manners and customs of animals. Alas! they have no critics. It is an art of which they know nothing—at least I know of no work of this kind in the archives of my animals. Perhaps my critic-friends know of some? Would they be kind enough to say so if they do, the sooner the better. No—there are no critics among animals. The wolf does not criticise the sheep—he eats it; not because he despises its art, but because he admires the flesh, and even the bones of this woolly animal which is so excellent in a stew. . . .

What we need is a discipline of iron, or of any other metal. Only the critics can impose such a discipline and see that it is obeyed—from a distance. . . . Anyone who disobeys is to be pitied . . . it is sad not to obey. But we must not obey our evil passions, even if they order us to themselves. How can we tell which are our evil passions? . . . By the pleasure we take in giving way to them and the PAIN THEY CAUSE THE CRITICS. They have no evil passions. How could they, poor fellows. They have no passions of any kind—none at all. Always calm and collected, they think only of their duty, which is to correct the faults of our poor world and make a decent income out of doing so with which to pay for their tobacco.

In his 'Cahiers d'un Mammifère'[35] (Notebooks of a Mammal) Satie again pokes fun at the critics: 'They are much more intelligent than is generally believed . . . That's why I want to become a critic—a little critic, only quite a tiny one, of course'. And again: 'What! Does he show no respect for the critics? Such a man can only be a Nobody (un pas grand'chose). You must be very careful not to have anything to do with him. . . .'

It was about this time, in the years that followed the First World War, that opinions were divided in France on the question of whether or not German music should be played. Satie, as was to be expected, was in the camp opposed to Saint-Saëns and critics like Laloy, and in favour of lifting the ban. 'We know', he wrote in these *Cahiers*, 'that Art has no Country—poor thing; she's not rich enough to have one . . . Why not, then, play Richard Strauss and Schönberg? Will you tell us that, dear Monsieur Laloy, you who know everything?'

It was almost axiomatic that in any controversy Satie would invariably be found on the 'unpopular' side—defending the rebels and attacking respected institutions, such as, for example, the Paris Conservatoire, and especially the famous 'Prix de Rome'. In a paper[36] ostensibly defending Albert Roussel (his old master at the Schola) against the charge of being 'only an amateur' (a charge brought against him by a former 'Prix de Rome') Satie inveighs against the absurd prestige attaching to this prize, and concludes sarcastically that since neither César Franck, d'Indy, Lalo, Chabrier nor Chausson were 'Prix de Rome' they must therefore be considered 'amateurs'. Why, he asks, must music alone of the arts be saddled with so much academic officialdom, when both painting and literature can dispense with it? 'The painters', he writes, 'with Manet, Cézanne, Picasso, Derain, Braque and others' broke away from these bad traditions and, risking everything, saved painting and artistic thinking generally from complete and absolute stultification. There is no "Prix de Rome" for literature, either; a writer does not have to have a University degree; even if he couldn't read, no one would think of blaming him. He would just be an illiterate writer, that's all. But for musicians it's different. They have a weakness for whatever is ridiculous. For example, Lavignac in his book *Music and Musicians* (p. 556) says: "The French school may be justly proud to number in its ranks such Masters as Gastinel, Colomer, Canoby, Mme la Comtesse de Grandval, Falkenberg, Mlle Augusta Holmès, Lepot-Delahaye,

[35] *Esprit Nouveau*. Paris. April 1921.   [36] *Les Feuilles Libres*, June-July 1922.

de Boisdefre, William Chaumet, etc." . . . (he must have done this for a wager) . . . You will notice that, fortunately, neither Chabrier, nor Debussy, nor Dukas are counted among these "masters of whom the French School can justly be proud . . ." And yet Lavignac was quite a good fellow, and his book well thought of in pedagogic circles . . . What? That, you see, is what our poor little children are being taught . . . ! How fortunate I am in not having any—not even one . . . I have always declared that in Art there is no Truth—no unique and absolute Truth, I mean. The kind that is forced upon one by Ministers, or a Senate or a Parliament or an Institute fills me with indignation and revolts me—although, after all, I don't really care, one way or the other.

'With a united voice I cry: "Long Live the Amateurs"!'

Elsewhere, had he not proclaimed with his customary clairvoyance and knack of expressing profound truths in the simplest terms: 'All great artists are amateurs', thus underlining the essential quality that distinguishes the true creative spirit from the mere technician. And with unfailing discernment (for we must admit his judgement on both his predecessors and his contemporaries was, in the main, both fair and perspicacious) Satie would separate the sheep from the goats, and generously bestow praise wherever he discerned merit. We know how he took up the cudgels on behalf of his young protégés, the 'Six', and continued to defend them when public opinion and that of 'the critics' began to turn against them; he also recognised Stravinsky as one of the greatest and most original artists of his time. Indeed in his study of the composer, 'Propos à Propos de Igor Stravinsky'[37] he did not hesitate to call him 'one of the most remarkable geniuses that music has ever known. The lucidity of his mind has set us free; his combative strength has won for us rights that we can never lose'.

This was written at a time when the production of *Mavra* in Paris was causing something of a sensation, since it seemed to show that Stravinsky was reverting to an elementary conception of the nature of opera and in so doing had produced a score which appeared to have no stylistic resemblance at all with any of his previous works. Satie, needless to say, did not agree with 'Messieurs les Critiques' whose complaints about *Mavra* seemed to him merely comic and proof of their complete inability to grasp the true significance of Stravinsky's latest volte-face.

It was also about this time that Stravinsky was experimenting

[37] *Les Feuilles Libres*, October-November 1922.

with his theories of 'mechanical interpretation' and writing music for the Pianola. Satie, while making it clear that the mechanical virtuosity of the pianola could never *take the place* of a human performer, (although the latter could never hope to equal it) yet gave Stravinsky the credit of having 'endowed music with a new element of enormous potentialities'. He pointed out that technically the pianola differs from the piano not so much as a photograph differs from a drawing but rather as a lithographic reproduction differs from the original; 'for the lithographer as it were plays the pianola, while the draughtsman plays the piano'.

He goes on to urge musicians to take an interest in this new method of registering music which, he opines, 'will develop the technique of writing music more swiftly and more surely than all the "pions" put together—or separately—could ever do'. And he concludes by describing Stravinsky as a 'magician'.

During the years 1912-1914 Satie contributed to the Review of the Société Internationale de Musique—S.I.M.—his celebrated *Mémoires d'un Amnésique*. The series consisted of six or seven short articles, including the one which has most often been quoted, 'La Journée du Musicien' (see p. 46). In the last year of his life he wrote for *Les Feuilles Libres* (Jan.-Feb., 1924), but under the same general title, an autobiographical sketch, half humorous, half serious, which he entitled *Recoins de ma Vie*. (See Appendix C.3.) This begins with the statement:

The origin of the Saties goes back, perhaps, to very distant times. Yes. On this point I can make no positive statement, nor a negative one either. . . . I do not know what the Saties did in the Hundred Years War; nor have I any information as to their attitude and the part they played in the Thirty Years War (one of our finest Wars). Let the memory of my old ancestors be undisturbed. . . . But to continue; I will return to this subject later. . . .

After a short adolescence I became quite a passable young man, no more than that. It was at this moment in my life that I began to think and write musically . . . Yes. An unfortunate idea, as it turned out, most unfortunate. For I soon began to show signs of an originality which was original, unpleasing, misplaced, anti-French, unnatural, etc., etc.

After that life became so unendurable that I decided to withdraw to my estates, and to spend my life in a tower of ivory—or of any material (of a metallic nature). It was thus that I developed a taste for misanthropy, cultivated hypochondria, and became the most melancholy of human beings. I was pitiful to behold—even through spectacles of controlled gold. . . . Yes.

And all this happened to me entirely owing to music. This art has done me more harm than good; it has caused me to quarrel with numerous honourable and estimable people, of the highest distinction and altogether 'comme il faut'. But to continue; I will return to this subject later. . . . Personally I am neither good nor bad. I oscillate, as you might say. Consequently I have never really harmed anyone—nor done anyone any good, for that matter.

Nevertheless I have a lot of enemies, faithful enemies, of course. Why? Chiefly because most of them don't know me—or only know of me at second-hand, or by hearsay (lies which are more than untrue). . . . A man cannot be perfect. I am not at all angry with them; they are the first victims of their own lack of conscience and perspicacity. Poor people; I am sorry for them.

But to continue; I will return to this subject later.

For the most part the *Mémoires* are either humorous or satirical or both; one of the most amusing instalments is that entitled *Ce que Je Suis* (What I am):

Everyone will tell you I am not a musician. (cf. O. Séré: *Musiciens français d'aujourd'hui*, p. 138). That is true. From the beginning of my career I classed myself among the 'phonometrographers'. My work is nothing but pure 'phonometry'. Take, for example, the *Fils des Etoiles*, or the *Morceaux en forme de Poire*, *En Habit de Cheval*, or the *Sarabandes*, and it will be seen at once that in the creation of these works musical ideas played no part at all. They are purely scientific. And as a matter of fact it gives me more pleasure to measure a sound than to hear it. With a phonometer in my hand I work happily and surely. What is there that I haven't weighed or measured? All Beethoven, all Verdi, etc. It's most interesting. The first time I used a phonoscope I examined a B flat of average dimensions. I can assure you I never in my life saw anything quite so repulsive. I had to call my servant to come and look at it.

On my phono-weighing-machine an ordinary F sharp, of a very common species, registered 93 kilograms. It came out of a very fat tenor whom I also weighed.[38]

Do you know how to clean sounds? It is rather a dirty process . . .;

[38]This recalls one of Satie's funniest sallies—rather in the vein of Stephen Leacock—concerning a piece of nonsense music scored for the following ridiculous instruments:

2 Flutes 'à piston' in F sharp	1 Siphon in C
1 Alto Overcoat in C	3 Keyboard |Trombones in D minor
1 Spring-lock in E	1 Double-Bass made of Skin in C
2 Slide-Clarinets in G minor	Chromatic Tub in B

'These instruments belong to the marvellous family of cephalophones, have a compass of thirty octaves, and are absolutely unplayable. An amateur in Vienna (Austria) in 1875 once tried to play the Siphon in C; after executing a trill, the instrument burst, broke his spinal column and scalped him completely. Since then no one has dared to avail themselves of the powerful resources of the cephalophones, and the State had to forbid these instruments to be taught in the Municipal Schools'.

as for indexing them, that is a very meticulous job which calls for good eyesight. Here we are in the phono-technical department. As regards sudden explosions of sound, which can be so disagreeable, cotton-wool in the ears attenuates the shock quite satisfactorily. This pertains to pyrophony.

In order to write my *Pièces Froides* I used a registering caleidophone. It only took me seven minutes. Then I called my servant in to let him hear them.

I think I can assert that phonology is superior to music. It's more varied and more remunerative—in fact I owe my fortune to it entirely. In any case, with a motodynamophone a moderately expert phonometrographer can easily note down more sounds than the most skilful musicians could do in the same time with the same expenditure of effort. That is why I have been able to write so much. One can therefore predict a future for philophony.[39]

Behind the jesting tone of this delightful bit of nonsense one can discern a note of bitterness: 'Everyone will tell you I am not a musician'—the bitterness of an essentially lonely man who is obliged to camouflage all his serious work in order to forestall the criticism he secretly fears. But by the exercise of his pen he was at least able to define his position, and, what is more, castigate the objects of his disapproval to his heart's content. For while still a young man he had developed a pretty gift for invective which he first exercised with considerable bravura, as we have seen, in the pages of his mysterious but short-lived journal, *Le Cartulaire*. Later on he inclined more and more to irony. The 'Eloge des Critiques', already quoted, is a good example of this, but of all his different styles the most typically Satiean is when he is giving free rein to his peculiar mock-serious brand of humour, 'pince-sans-rire', as for example, in his essay on 'Intelligence and Musical Appreciation among Animals' (from the *Mémoires d'un Amnésique*).

He begins by blaming humans for having neglected the education of animals, their 'concitoyens', who have never been taught about art or literature or natural or moral science:

Homing pigeons are not trained for their profession by being made to study geography; fish are given no opportunities of studying oceanography; oxen, sheep and calves know nothing about the superior organisation of the modern slaughter-house, nor are they aware of the nutritive function they have to perform in the society which man has organised for himself. Few animals learn anything from humans. The dog, the mule, the horse, the ass, the parrot, the blackbird and a few others are the only animals to receive even the

[39]The French text appears as Appendix C.4.

most rudimentary instruction. . . . As to music? Well, horses have learned to dance, and spiders have been known to stay under a piano during an entire concert, a concert organised for their benefit by a reputed master of the keyboard. But after that? Nothing. Only very occasionally we hear of musical starlings, or of crows with an ear for melody, or of the harmonic ingenuity of the owl who accompanies himself by tapping on his own stomach—a purely artificial procedure and yielding only a scant polyphony.

As for the nightingale, so often cited, the extent of her musical knowledge would make even the most ignorant among her hearers shrug his shoulders. Not only is her voice not properly 'placed'; she is completely ignorant on the subject of key, tonality, modality and time. But perhaps the nightingale has talent? That is possible, even certain. But it can be stated that her artistic culture lags behind her natural gifts, and that this voice of which she is so proud is only a very inferior instrument having no value in itself.[40]

In yet another instalment of the *Mémoires*, entitled 'Parfait Entourage', Satie amuses himself with a description of his collection of 'fakes', which included a magnificent 'faux Rembrandt', 'delicious to press with the eyes like a fat, but too green fruit'. There was also a 'delightful Portrait attributed to an Unknown Painter', and an 'imitation Teniers', 'pièce rare entre toutes'.

And yet, [he goes on] what eclipses these masterly works, crushing them with the formidable weight of the majesty of genius, dimming them by its own dazzling radiance is—a forged MS of Beethoven— a sublime apocryphal Symphony by the Master which I bought piously ten years ago—I think it was. Of all the works of this grandiose composer this 10th Symphony, still unknown, is one of the most sumptuous. Its proportions are as vast as those of a Palace; the ideas are fresh and plentiful; the developments clear and correct.

It was necessary for this symphony to exist—the number 9 is quite unlike Beethoven. He liked the decimal system: 'I have ten fingers, you see', he would explain.

Some people who came to absorb this masterpiece with filial piety and attentive and meditative ears quite unreasonably judged it to be an inferior conception of Beethoven, and said so. They even went further.

Beethoven could never in any circumstances be inferior to himself. His technique and form are always august, even in the smallest detail. Nothing elementary could be compared to him. He is not to be frightened by any forgery involving his artistic personality. Do you suppose that a famous athlete, whose skill and strength have long been acclaimed, lowers himself by being able to carry with ease a

[40]The French text is given as Appendix C.5.

simple bouquet of mixed tulips and jasmine? Is he diminished in any way if in addition he is assisted by a child? . . .

We have seen how in the *Piège de Méduse* Satie was his own librettist. There is also in existence an unpublished fragment (in MS)[41] of a scene he once wrote for a shadow-play which he planned to write in collaboration with M. Roland-Manuel, which is very characteristic.

The personage in this scene has evidently been arrested and put in prison for some reason, and is bewailing his sad fate: 'I shan't be able to go to the café, or go shooting, or visit my Notary, or go in a bus, or fishing at Montreuil, or go to the theatre, or the races or to the sea-side' ('aux bains de mer de famille'. Having written 'bains de mer' Satie cannot resist adding 'de famille', 'mer' suggesting 'mère de famille'. This was a favourite trick of his in writing).

Suddenly, however, he reflects that he has an alibi—'un tout-tout petit-tit t'alibi'. 'Can't I say', he asks himself, 'that I was beside myself (hors de moi) and far (more than two thousand miles) from imagining that I was committing a crime? . . . I am saved! I am my own saviour and propose for myself a well-deserved vote of thanks. What's more, I can claim a reward of 25 francs. I'm off to collect it. Waiter! My hat and stick!'

Somewhat similar in spirit is a little sketch which formed part of the *Mémoires d'un Amnésique* published under the title of 'Choses de Théâtre'. The text of this little essay in the absurd is as follows:

I have always wanted to write a lyric drama on the following specific subject:

At that time I was going in for alchemy. Alone in my laboratory one day I was resting. Outside, a leaden sky, livid and sinister—a horror!

I was feeling mournful, without knowing why; almost afraid, though for no apparent reason. It then occurred to me to amuse myself by counting on my fingers, slowly, from one to 260,000.

This I did, but only succeeded in becoming more and more bored. Rising from my chair I went to take a magic nut and put it carefully in a casket of alpaca bone studded with seven diamonds.

Immediately a stuffed bird flew out; a monkey's skeleton ran away; a sow's skin climbed up the wall. Then night descended, covering everything up and abolishing shapes.

But someone is knocking on the door—the door nearest to the Median talismans, the talismans which were sold to me by a Polynesian maniac. What can it be? Oh God! do not abandon thy servant.

[41]Kindly communicated by M. Roland-Manuel.

He has certainly sinned, but now he repents. Pardon him, I beseech thee. Now the door is opening, opening—opening like an eye; a silent, shapeless creature is coming nearer, coming nearer, coming nearer. . . . Not a single drop of sweat remains on my terrorised skin; moreover I am extremely thirsty, extremely thirsty.

Out of the shadows comes a voice: 'Sir, I think I must have double sight'.

I do not recognise this voice. It goes on: 'Sir, it is I, it is only I'. 'Who are you?' I mutter in terror. 'It's I, your servant. I think I must have double sight. Did you not place with care a magic nut in a casket of alpaca bone studded with seven diamonds?' Suffocated, I could only answer: 'Yes, my friend. But how did you know?' He drew nearer, gliding darkly through the night. I could feel him trembling. No doubt he was afraid I was going to shoot him. Then, with a sob, like a little child, he murmured: 'I saw you through the key-hole.'

Chapter X

His Character

It has been necessary to quote somewhat extensively from Satie's published writings in order to become acquainted with that particular side of his peculiar and composite genius. We have seen how the rather ponderous invective with which, in his early crusading days, he used so effectively to bludgeon his adversaries, was replaced in his more mature writing by the razor-edge of irony, of which he was a master. The other chief weapons in his literary armoury were humour, wit, and fantasy, the whole mixture leavened with a dash of poetic lyricism.

As can be imagined his epistolary style, too, was lively and capricious. He had a preference for the letter-card or the 'pneumatique' which he used freely and frequently, often, it would seem, merely as the vehicle for some wisecrack or humorous comment on nothing in particular. For instance, he writes to a lady on a post card bearing his own portrait (by Frueh): 'My dear Lady, the sun has gone away from Arcueil. He has gone to cook himself somewhere else. What a character! The wind has been here for several days. He is just passing through. It is amazing how strong he has become for his age . . .'

One of Satie's peculiarities was his detestation of the sun— 'Ce cochon-là' he would call it, 'a brute and a criminal who, not content with toasting our prison windows amuses himself by wickedly burning up the peasants' crops. What a crashing bore he is! He looks like a great calf with a head as red as a cock's! He ought to be ashamed of himself'. Another time, in fixing a rendezvous at a café at half-past six he specifies that he means half-past six in the evening, because: 'J'aime mieux le soir que le matin, si vous le permettez. Le soir est moins matinal. C'est connu'.

Again, speaking of a friend who had had an unsuccessful day's fishing: 'He didn't catch anything, thanks to the wind which came to visit him and broke all his lines. The fish were furious, and would have been very nasty fried . . .'

There is no evidence that he ever wrote or spoke his mother's native language, though he introduced English words and phrases into some of the commentaries with which his piano pieces are besprinkled; and in one of his letters, where he is querying some signature, he writes: 'Ouate hisse zatte? (mots anglais)'.

His conversation, when in congenial company, must have been extremely entertaining. In his deep, rather drawling voice, interrupted from time to time by fits of laughter which he would stifle behind a hand spread over his mouth and beard, he would mingle wisecracks and wisdom, and invest the most ordinary conversation with an air of profound mystery. Bowler-hatted, with his umbrella under his arm and on occasions the stem of an enormous clay pipe emerging from his pocket (he belonged to the 'Club de la Clay-Pipe' which had no members but three chairmen, of whom he was one) the 'bon maître d'Arcueil' would plod indefatigably from one end of Paris to the other, often alone, sometimes accompanied by a boon companion whom he had inveigled to 'see him home'. It was no rare thing for him to leave Montmartre at about 2 a.m., trudge across Paris to his southerly suburb where he would arrive with the sun; have a quick wash and brush-up and then turn round and set off again for the Butte where he would arrive in time for lunch. On these nocturnal expeditions it was his custom to carry a hammer in his pocket as a defence against possible molestation in some of the less salubrious quarters of the city which he had to traverse on his way to Arcueil. A good deal of his composing was done on café tables. Satie was something of a gourmet and a voracious eater. As Cocteau said: 'He had a flair for good inns and liked to live where life ferments'. He was also not averse to alcohol in which he occasionally indulged not wisely but too well. 'Jeunes gens', he wrote, 'n'allez pas au café; écoutez la voix grave d'un homme qui y a beaucoup été—mais qui ne le regrette pas, le monstre!' (But that advice, he confessed, was given 'pour avoir l'air respectable . . .').

Mercredi 5 janvier 1916

Chère Madame —— Pourriez-vous me confier —pour deux ou trois jours —— le recueil des cinq russes (Rimsky, César Cui, Borodine, etc...) sur :

[musical notation] etc... ?

Cet ouvrage, publié en Bochie, est, bien que russe, introuvable, & j'en ai le plus pressant besoin. Roland l'a dans sa musique russe.

Je passerai, si vous le permettez, demain jeudi, vers 14 h.—14 h.½, anciennement 2 h.—2 h.½.

Tout d'avance.

Mille choses à Monsieur Dreyfus.

Respectueusement

[signature]

P.S. Monsieur Labori (est-ce l'orthographe ?) est très sympathique. Avez-vous des nouvelles nouvelles de Roland ? J'ai vu Stravinsky : l'opinion russe feront encore un an de guerre. C'est leur mort, "le demi". On en aura pour son argent !

A typical Satie letter-card

' Si je suis français ? Bien sûr—pourquoi voulez vous qu'un homme de mon âge ne soit pas français ? Vous me surprenez . . . '

His dress, in later life, was curiously correct and conventional; he might have been taken for a bank clerk or a notary or a schoolmaster, not for a musician. His linen and his person were always spotlessly clean; one of his idiosyncracies was that he never washed his hands with soap, but invariably used pumice-stone.

Innumerable stories are told of his eccentricities and of his delight in jokes and mystifications of all kinds—a legacy Erik had inherited from his uncle 'Sea-Bird' who as we have seen had been inhabited by the same Puckish spirit of pure fantasy. Once he was approached by a poor down-and-out who was in the last stages of despair. On learning that this was due to his inability to find work Satie had an inspiration. 'Why don't you take up medicine?' he asked. 'Medicine?' stammered the other. 'But you can't become a doctor just like that—you have to pass exams and things, get a diploma . . .' 'Not at all. Quite unnecessary. Diplomas are even a hindrance, if anything. The profession is open to anyone, and you can earn a lot of money at it'. 'You think so?' 'Think so? I'm sure of it. To prove it, I'll make you a present of my practice now'. 'Well, if that's the case', said the other, 'I'll have a shot at it. Thanks for the tip'. And the poor fellow shuffled away, full of new courage and hope. One can almost hear Satie's chuckle as he muttered his 'Bonjou', bonjou' ' behind his beard.

He must have chuckled, too, when he brought off his celebrated cognac trick in the cafés. It was the custom at that time to serve cognac in small graduated *carafons* of a conical shape and divided into three sections, each containing what was supposed to be a normal dose. But Satie had observed that the bottom section contained a slightly larger dose than the other two. He would therefore ask for an extra glass to be brought, explaining to the mystified waiter that as he only wanted to consume the bottom portion of the carafe he would pour the remainder away. When told he ought to 'take it as it comes', and that if he wanted the bottom portion he had only to drink the others first—'Not at all', he would gravely reply; 'I prefer the underneath portion because it hasn't been exposed to the air; and, what's more, I am legally entitled to drink only the *middle* portion if I choose; and if I don't it's solely so as not to cause you any inconvenience'. Whereupon he would pour away the two top portions and empty the remainder into his coffee.[42]

[42]Both above anecdotes from 'The Velvet Gentleman' by Georges Auriol, *La Revue Musicale*, March, 1924.

Satie never married. 'Je suis un homme', he used to say, 'que les femmes ne comprennent pas'. It is equally doubtful whether he understood women or really liked them. Yet his youth was marked by at least one 'affaire du cœur', idyllic while it lasted, in which his partner was Suzanne Valadon, afterwards to become famous as a painter and the mother of a still more famous painter son—Maurice Utrillo.

But he was too uncouth in later life to look or hope for successes in that quarter; and his total lack of any real understanding of feminine psychology was revealed on one occasion in a most surprising way. Wishing to end a liaison he felt had lasted long enough, instead of notifying the lady he notified the police! And so her first intimation of this cooling of his affections was when she found a police guard posted outside his house with orders to prevent her entry; he had simply told the police he did not wish to be molested . . . There are many ways of breaking off attachments of this kind; the method chosen by Satie may have been original; it was certainly quite fantastically inelegant.

All of which goes to show that as the modern psychologist would say Satie was 'maladjusted' to his surroundings and to his epoch; he was, in fact, as Debussy had observed, 'égaré dans ce siècle'. He was essentially a solitary, withdrawn within himself, living largely in a world of his own construction. So many oddities, so many contradictions in his character can hardly otherwise be explained. The solitariness of his music, too, is what we notice first; it is so difficult to 'connect' it with anything familiar —in spite of the fact that the composer was in reality acutely 'aware' of everything going on round him. But with this awareness went a strange indifference; and that is the reason, in the words of one perspicacious critic[43], why 'there is no music like it; because never before has the artist felt so apathetic—not antipathetic, which is a different matter—to humanity as to make such a strange achievement possible. Only a very remarkable personality could attain to the degree of impersonality which makes this music, not one man's loneliness, but an aspect of the modern consciousness, transformed into sound'.

'An aspect of the modern consciousness'—a suggestive remark in the light of which one would like now, after having sketched a portrait of the man, to attempt a final estimate of the real nature of Satie's contribution to the music of our time.

[43]W. H. Mellers. *Studies in Contemporary Music*. Dobson, 1948.

Chapter XI

The Significance of Satie in Contemporary Music

'Satie a protégé sa musique comme du bon vin.
Il n'a jamais remué la bouteille'.

COCTEAU

THE AMOUNT OF CONTROVERSY of an extra-musical nature aroused by the personality, opinions, mode of life, literary and other associations of Erik Satie has led some observers to affirm that his 'case' belongs properly to the domain of literary rather than of musical criticism. It is of course undeniable that many of the factors that have contributed to the building up of the Satie 'Legend' have been only indirectly connected with his music; indeed, one of the main problems with which his biographers are faced is how to disentangle the music and the musician from all the extraneous associations with which they are encrusted and overlaid. Nevertheless, even though Satie's output in the main may be significant more for what it hints at than for what it actually achieves, yet many of his works, I maintain, have an intrinsic value of their own which is indisputable, and indeed, unique. The *Gymnopédies*, *Gnossiennes*, *Airs à faire Fuir*, *Sports et Divertissements* and *Nocturnes*, among the piano works; *Socrate* and the ballet *Parade* (to make a quick selection) are outstanding and cannot be ignored by any student of contemporary music. As to their 'contemporaneity', in the sense of their being an expression of 'an aspect of the modern consciousness', Georges Auric, in a passage already quoted[44], seems to hint at this when he says that Satie's works, 'although written without reference to the prevailing taste and style of the day . . . have in reality *anticipated* those tastes and styles . . . with the most astonishing precision. . . .' Satie, in fact, gave expression to what was *latent* in the consciousness of the world in which he lived; in other words he was the interpreter to the world of its own subconscious (aesthetic) dreams and aspirations. In the *Sarabandes* of 1887 he foreshadowed the lines on which modern harmony was going to be developed by Debussy and other great twentieth-century composers; the nostalgic *Gymnopédies*, written at the same period, but entirely without reference to either Wagner or Franck, point the way to that return to the old French traditions and a generally modal style which were exemplified later in the works of Debussy and Ravel; and then, in the heyday of

[44]See p. 51.

Impressionism, about 1912, came the *Préludes Flasques* which in their linear austerity heralded the 'neo-classic' vogue which was to dominate Western music during the nineteen-twenties. Moreover, *Parade* (1917) was certainly the precursor of a good deal of the 'mechanistic' music which was a feature of the post-First World War years right up to 1939; while the *Piège de Méduse*, composed in 1913, anticipated Dada by some three years just as surely as the *Heures Séculaires et Instantanées* of 1914, especially taken in conjunction with their accompanying text, can now be seen to be of purely Surrealist inspiration. *Socrate*, on the other hand, has a quality of timelessness which is no less remarkable. And, of course—perhaps the most significant pointer of all—we must never forget that while the young Debussy was still working on Wagnerian lines on a libretto of Catulle Mendès (*Rodrigue et Chimène*), Erik Satie was already planning his *Princesse Maleine*, only, as he confided to Debussy, 'did not know how to obtain Maeterlinck's permission'. Soon afterwards it was Debussy who had obtained Maeterlinck's permission, and had started to write *Pelléas et Mélisande* . . . . No one is going to pretend that Satie's opera would have been in any way comparable to *Pelléas*; what is important is that he should have been thinking at all on those lines at that time. In any case, the incident decided his future line of action. As Cocteau has pointed out, 'Satie showed his genius by recognising, already in 1896, that *Pelléas* was a masterpiece, and by being generous (and clever) enough to admit that his friend Claude had hit the bull's-eye. You remember what he said after the success of *Pelléas*?—"I must find another line; if I don't, I'm lost".' What that 'other line' ('autre chose') was I have tried in these pages to expound. And whatever may be the ultimate verdict of posterity, the extreme originality and high degree of invention displayed in so much of Satie's almost disarmingly unassuming œuvre cannot fail to strike any but the most prejudiced observer. M. Charles Koechlin compares him to Kipling's 'Cat that walked by Himself', and rightly ascribes to his music all the virtues of the cat—namely: 'its elegant litheness, the sobriety and restraint of its movements, the accuracy of its paw-work when engaged in crafty play, its discreet sensibility which eludes the common man's perception, and finally, and above all, its instinctive and absolute independence'. And the greatest of these outstanding feline virtues is—independence, Satie's most marked characteristic. Always he went his own way, without ever troubling his head about what the 'other fellow' was doing or about to do. But the 'other fellow' frequently shot a sideways glance at Satie, to see what *he* might be up to. For you never knew—it might after all be worth while to keep an eye on him—or even to take a leaf out of his copy-book. And so consciously or unconsciously the famous 'influence' came to make itself felt. Few composers of our day in fact escaped it altogether; many have openly acknowledged it. Milhaud and Poulenc both have; so has Ravel, who confessed to a friend that the musician who had had the greatest influence on him was Erik Satie. (Consider, for example, 'La Belle et la Bête' from *Ma Mère l'Oye*.) Ravel furthermore bracketed Chabrier and Satie together as the two French composers who seemed to him to be the most 'necessary'. In Stravinsky, too, can we fail to notice a page here or a passage there where the shadow of Satie has not fallen? The Introduction to *Mavra*, for example, contains unmistakably Satiean foot-prints; while the First 'Variation' in the Sonata for Two Pianos might almost be a transcription of the First *Gymnopédie* (the chording in the second Piano part is practically identical with the accompaniment figure in the first *Gymnopédie:*

But concrete examples are not indispensable: the spirit of Satie can be 'felt', perhaps better than it can be demonstrated, animating so much of modern music of which he was, in a very real sense, the prophet. A lesser musician than that other great figure in twentieth-century music, Debussy, but a great prophet. For in Satie were the germs of the new music; and while Debussy summed up his own epoch, Satie foreshadowed the next. This was the miracle referred to by Milhaud, by virtue of which 'Satie remained eternally the youngest of the young while his works invariably satisfied the aspirations of the latest comers. . . . He knew well that a younger generation would always stand up for him and love him for the perfection of his music and for his complete and uncompromising sincerity'.

But if the young had faith in Satie, he returned the compliment not only in words, but, as we have seen, in deeds. Always he championed youth and new movements—'La Jeunesse présente et future se chargera de mettre les choses au point' he wrote two years before he died. And he gave this definition of what he meant by *esprit nouveau*: 'it teaches us to aim at an emotive simplicity and a firmness of utterance enabling sonorities and rhythms to assert themselves clearly, unequivocal in design and accent, and contrived in a spirit of humility and renunciation'.[45]

Does not this express admirably the ideal by which a great deal of contemporary music is—or at least professes to be—animated today? Satie was right once more. 'L'avenir', he wrote, 'me donnera raison. N'ai-je pas été déjà bon prophète?'

And so we take leave of one of the most intriguing figures in musical history—a composer whose name is known to many but his music to few—a composer whom no musician would rank higher than a 'petit maître', and yet one to whom some of the greatest of his peers have paid homage, seeing in him a bold and lucid visionary, a humble but serious practician, but above all a kind of inspired magician in whose hands music could be made to undergo, at a wave of his wand, the most surprising and unprecedented transformations. No other composer has had this power of doing the completely unexpected with music; while few have served their art with greater devotion and abnegation or with clearer views as to its possibilities and potentialities. Admittedly the field he worked in was a restricted one; but within those limits, which were largely self-imposed, and in spite of personal limitations of which he was only too well aware, the work he did was that of a pioneer. Everything he came into contact with was vivified by his touch; everyone who approached him was stimulated by his ideas. Like Socrates, he went about in a questing spirit arousing with his gad-fly's sting the hostility of the complacent, but winning the admiration and affection of all those who saw in him not only an artist of rare integrity, but a sage who concealed his wisdom under an engaging mask of mockery and Puckish humour. It has been the object of these pages to reveal, in what I hope is the right perspective, the real nature of his achievement, and to show why we have good cause to see in Erik Satie the forerunner and herald of much that is significant in the music of our time.

[45] *Les Feuilles Libres*, March 1923.

Appendix A

Translation of letters on pp. 24, 27 and 28.

Paris, this fourteenth day of the month of August in the year of '92.
Master Editor,

Truly it doth amaze me that I a poor wretch, having no thoughts but for my art alone, should continually be proclaimed and hailed as Initiator in music of the disciples of Master Joseph Péladan. This grieves and offends me sorely inasmuch as were I to be the pupil of whomsoever, methinks that whomsoever would be none other than myself; the more so since I hold to the belief that Master Péladan, for all the fullness of his learning, could never make disciples either in music, painting or in aught besides. Wherefore I declare the aforesaid Master Péladan, whom I hold truly in full respect and fitting deference, has never in any wise exercised authority over the independence of my Aesthetic, and stands to me in the relation, not of Teacher but of Colleague, thus differing in no wise from my old friends Masters J. P. Contamine de Latour and Albert Tinchant.

Before Holy Mary, Mother of Our Lord Jesus, Third Person of the Divine Trinity, I have spoken and declared, without hatred or evil intent, the View I take of such an intention; and I swear before the Fathers of the Holy Church that in all this I have not sought to do injury to, nor do I cherish any grievance against my friend Master Péladan.

Be so good, Master Editor, as to accept the humble salutations of a poor wretch, having no thoughts but for his Art alone, and grieved to have to deal with a question that causes him so much pain.

ERIK SATIE

'Abbatiale', May 2nd, 1895. Erik Satie, 'Parcier et Maître de Chapelle', to M. Gauthier-Villars

Combating his swollen-headedness and in defence of Magnificent Things

Sir,

The sacred character of Art makes the critic's functions all the more delicate; you degrade these functions by the inexcusable lack of respect and incompetence with which you perform them. Be advised through God that all thinking men unite in condemning you for wishing to touch things that are far above you, in order to debase them.

The demoniacal dragon of presumptuousness has made you blind. You committed blasphemy in your judgment of Wagner who, for you, remains the Unknown and the Infinite. As for Me, I can curse

131

him at My leisure; My dynastic melodies, My athletic appearance
and the asceticism of My life empower Me to do this. With these
words I command you to absent yourself from My person, and to
absorb yourself, in sorrow and in silence, in painful meditation. .

ERIK SATIE.

May 14 . . . to M. Gauthier-Villars

Expressing all the scorn which attaches to his person

Envious of reputations too exalted for your inferior state, the
careers of the great and their continued triumphs incite you to pour
out the gall with which you attempt to defile everything you
approach. I have spoken of Wagner and of your crass ignorance;
you reply with extravagant word-stringing, and with what a writer
less praiseworthy than praised, Victor Hugo, called the excrements
of the mind. Your breath exhales falsehood; from your lips issue
forth boldness and indecency. Your turpitude has recoiled upon
you, for it has made plain to even the meanest intelligence the full
extent of your unsurpassed boorishness. What is there for a normal,
healthy person to say in the presence of so much vanity working
for such trivial ends? I can but ignore the villainies committed by
a buffoon; but I am obliged to raise a hand to overthrow the
Oppressors of the Church and of Art—all those who, like you, have
never known self-respect. As to those who hope to get the better of
Me by means of terrorism and abuse, let them know that I am
determined and fearless. Does Gauthier-Villars, that repulsive
"Circus usherette" (allusion to his pseudonym) that false comedian
calling himself "Willy", threefold monument of abject ignominy,
imagine that because he is a sordid mercenary of the pen, a per-
petual degradation amongst the lowest of the low, I should not dare
to do to him what I would dare to do to the direst evil-doer? If he
does, he is mistaken.

ERIK SATIE.

Appendix B

USPUD

ballet chrétien en trois actes de j.p. contamine de la tour; musique d'erik satie. présenté au théâtre national de l'opéra le 20 dec. 1892. personnage unique: uspud.
spiritualités: l'église chrétienne, saints et saintes, martyrs et confesseurs, le christ en croix, messagers celestes des sept ordres; démonialités.

Acte I

une plage déserte; au milieu une statue; au loin la mer.

USPUD vêtu à la persane.

uspud revient du supplice des chrétiens et rapporte des reliques. il les entasse au pied de la statue et les brûle; la fumée qui s'en dégage se change en séraphins qui s'évanouissent dans l'espace.

un coup de tonnerre formidable retentit; la statue tombe en morceaux. uspud est consterné.

tout à coup le ciel devient blanc. une femme d'une grande beauté, couverte d'une tunique d'or et la poitrine percée d'un poignard, apparaît devant uspud et lui tend les bras. c'est l'église chrétienne.

uspud, étonné, prend du sable et s'en frotte les yeux.

sonnerie de trompettes. defilé aérien de martyrs qui maudissent uspud.

uspud ramasse des pierres et les jette à l'église chrétienne; les pierres se changent en globes de feu. fureur d'uspud. il prend une pierre plus grosse, qui éclate avec fracas; des flammes surgissent et de leur sein s'échappent des étoiles. grande convulsion de la nature.

fin du premier acte

Acte II
la maison d'USPUD

USPUD implore ses dieux lares

des démons surgissent et disparaissent aussitôt; ils affectent le forme d'hommes contrefaits avec des têtes d'animaux tels que chien, chacal, tortue, chèvre, poisson, lynx, tigre-loup, bœuf, bécasse de mer, licorne, mouton, antilope, fourmi, araignée, gnou, serpent, agouti-bouc bleu, babouin, cuculu, crabe, albatros, pâcre, autruche, taupe, secrétaire, vieux taureau, chenille rouge, bonti, pogos, sanglier, crocodile, buffle, etc.

uspud effrayé veut s'enfuir, mais les démons l'entourent et le bousculent; il essaie de se broyer la tête, mais les murs reculent et suintent le sang. dans l'air on voit la vision d'un tribunal païen, devant lequel on torture les victimes. uspud, dans son angoisse, implore le ciel.

l'église chrétienne apparâit de nouveau, blanche comme la neige et transparente comme le cristal; des lotus naissent sous ses pieds. elle retire le poignard de sa poîtrine et l'enfonce dans celle d'uspud, qui entre en extase. en même temps un crucifix gigantesque sort de terre et s'élève vers le ciel, entrainant à sa suite l'église chrétienne. on entend les chœur des anges, archanges, séraphins, chérubins, trônes, puissances et dominations qui chantent un hymne au très-haut. une grand lumière enveloppe uspud; il tombe à genoux, en se frappant la poitrine. il est converti.

fin du second acte

Acte III

le sommet d'une montagne; au dessus un crucifix.

uspud vêtu de bure, est prosterné devant le crucifix; pendant longtemps il prie et pleure.

quand il relève la tête, le christ détache son bras droit de la croix, bénit uspud et disparait. l'esprit-saint pénètre uspud.

défilé de saints et saintes: saint cléophème crache ses dents dans sa main; sainte micanar les yeux dans un plateau; le bienheureux marcomir, les jambes calcinées; saint induciomare le corps percé de flêches; saint chassebaigre, confesseur, en robe violette; saint lumore avec un glaive; saint gebu avec des tenailles rougies; sainte glunde avec une roue; saint krenou avec un mouton; saint japuis, le front ouvert et des colombes s'en echappent; saint umbeuse filant la laine; le bien heureux melou l'estropié; saint vequin l'écorché; saint purine la déchaussée; saint plan moine prêcheur; sainte lenu avec une hache. leurs voix appellent uspud au martyre.

une soif inextinguible de souffrance le pénètre. il déchire sa robe de bure et apparaît vêtu de la tunique blanche des néophytes. il se remet en prière.

une légion de démons surgit de tous les côtés. ils revêtent des formes monstrueuses: chiens noirs avec une corne d'or sur le front; corps de poissons avec des têtes et des ailes d'oiseaux; géants au chef de taureau, soufflant du feu par les narines.

uspud recommande son esprit au seigneur, puis se livre aux démons qui le déchirent avec fureur.

l'église chrétienne apparaît, éblouissante de clarté et escortée de deux anges, portant des palmes et des couronnes. elle prend l'âme d'uspud dans ses bras et l'enlève vers le christ, qui rayonne dans le ciel.

fin du troisième acte

RIDEAU

Appendix C

I

MÉMOIRES D'UN AMNÉSIQUE
LA JOURNÉE DU MUSICIEN (fragment)

L'artiste doit régler sa vie.
Voici l'horaire précis de mes actes journaliers:
Mon lever: à 7h.18; inspiré: de 10h.23 à 11h.47. Je déjeune à 12h.11 et quitte la table à 12h.14.
Salutaire promenade à cheval, dans le fond de mon parc: de 13h.19 à 14h.53. Autre inspiration: de 15h.12 à 16h.07.
Ocupations diverses (escrime, réflexions, immobilité, visites, contemplation, dextérité, natation, etc. . . .): de 16 h.21 à 18h.47.
Le dîner est servi à 19h.16 et terminé à 19h.20. Viennent des lectures symphoniques, à haute voix: de 20h.09 à 21h.59.
Mon coucher a lieu régulièrement à 22h.37. Hebdomadairement, réveil en sursaut à 3h.19 (le mardi).

Je ne mange que des aliments blancs: des œufs, du sucre, des os rapés; de la graisse d'animaux morts; du veau, du sel, des noix de coco, du poulet cuit dans de l'eau blanche; des moisissures de fruits, du riz, des navets; du boudin camphré, des pâtes, du fromage (blanc), de la salade de coton et de certains poissons (sans la peau).

Je fais bouillir mon vin, que je bois froid avec du jus de fuchsia. J'ai bon appétit; mais je ne parle jamais en mangeant, de peur de m'étrangler.

Je respire avec soin (peu à la fois). Je danse très rarement. En marchant, je me tiens par les côtés et regarde fixement derrière moi.

D'aspect très sérieux, si je ris, c'est sans le faire exprès. Je m'en excuse toujours et avec affabilité.

Je ne dors que d'un œil; mon sommeil est très dur. Mon lit est rond, percé d'un trou pour le passage de la tête. Toutes les heures, un domestique prend ma température et m'en donne une autre.

Depuis longtemps, je suis abonné à un journal de modes. Je porte un bonnet blanc, des bas blancs et un gilet blanc.

Mon médecin m'a toujours dit de fumer. Il ajoute à ses conseils:
— Fumez, mon ami: sans cela, un autre fumera à votre place.

ERIK SATIE.

S.I.M.   15 Février 1913.

2

ÉLOGE DES CRITIQUES

Ce n'est pas le hasard qui m'a fait choisir ce sujet — C'est la reconnaissance, car je suis aussi reconnaissant que reconnaissable.

J'ai fait, l'an dernier, plusieurs conférences sur 'l'Intelligence et la Musicalité chez les animaux'.

Aujourd'hui, je vous parlerai de 'l'Intelligence et la Musicalité chez les critiques'. C'est à peu près le même thème, avec modifications, bien entendu.

Des amis m'ont dit que ce sujet était ingrat.

Pourquoi ingrat? Il n'y a là aucune ingratitude; du moins, je ne vois pas où elle se tient: Je ferai donc froidement l'éloge des critiques.

On ne connaît pas assez les critiques; on ignore ce qu'ils ont fait, ce qu'ils sont capables de faire. En un mot, ils sont aussi méconnus que les animaux; bien que, comme ceux-ci, ils aient leur utilité.

Oui, ils ne sont pas seulement les créateurs de l'Art critique, ce Maître de tous les Arts, ils sont les premiers penseurs du Monde, les libres-penseurs mondains, si l'on peut dire.

Du reste, c'est un critique qui posa pour le *Penseur* de Rodin. J'ai appris ce fait par un critique, il y a quinze jours, trois semaines au plus. Cela m'a fait plaisir, beaucoup de plaisir. Rodin avait un faible pour les critiques, un grand faible . . .

Leurs conseils lui étaient chers, très chers, trop chers, hors de prix.

Il y a trois sortes de critiques: ceux qui ont de l'importance; ceux qui en ont moins; ceux qui n'en ont pas du tout. Les deux dernières sortes n'existent pas: tous les critiques ont de l'importance.

*   *   *

Physiquement, le critique est d'aspect grave. C'est un type dans le genre du contrebasson. Il est lui-même un centre, un centre de gravité. S'il rit, il ne rit que d'un œil, soit du bon, soit du mauvais. Toujours très aimable avec les Dames, il tient les Messieurs à distance, tranquillement. En un mot, il est assez intimidant, bien que très agréable à voir. C'est un homme sérieux, sérieux comme un Boudda, un boudin noir, évidemment. La médiocrité, l'incapacité, ne se rencontrent pas chez les critiques. Un critique médiocre, ou incapable serait la risée de ses confrères; il lui serait impossible d'exercer sa profession, son sacerdoce, veux-je dire, car il lui faudrait quitter son pays même natal; et toutes les portes lui seraient fermées; sa vie ne serait plus qu'un long supplice, terrible de monotonie.

L'Artiste n'est qu'un rêveur, en somme; le critique, lui, a la conscience du réel, et la sienne, en plus. Un artiste peut être imité;

le critique est inimitable, et impayable. Comment pourrait-on imiter un critique? Je me le demande. Du reste, l'intérêt serait mince, très mince. Nous avons l'original, IL NOUS SUFFIT. Celui qui a dit que la critique était aisée n'a pas dit quelque chose de bien remarquable. C'est même honteux d'avoir dit cela: on devrait le poursuivre, pendant au moins un kilomètre ou deux.

L'homme qui écrivit une telle chose. Peut-être le regretta-t-il ce propos? C'est possible, c'est à souhaiter, C'EST CERTAIN.

* * *

Le cerveau du critique est un magasin, un grand magasin. On y trouve de tout: orthopédie, sciences, literie, arts, couvertures de voyage, grands choix de mobiliers, papier à lettres français et étrangers, articles pour fumeurs, ganterie, parapluies, lainages, chapeaux, sports, cannes, optique, parfumerie, etc. . . . Le critique sait tout, voit tout, dit tout, entend tout, touche à tout, remue tout, mange de tout, confond tout, et n'en pense pas moins. Quel homme!! Qu'on se le dise!! ! Tous nos articles sont garantis! ! ! Pendant les chaleurs, la marchandise est dans l'intérieur! ! ! DANS L'INTÉRIEUR DU CRITIQUE! ! Voyez! ! Rendez-vous compte, mais ne touchez pas! ! ! C'est unique, incroyable.

Le critique est aussi une vigie, une bouée, peut-on ajouter. Il signale les récifs qui bordent les côtes de l'Esprit Humain. Près de ces côtes, de ces fausses côtes, le critique veille superbe de clairvoyance de loin, il a un peu l'air d'une borne, mais d'une borne sympathique intelligente.

Comment parvient-il à cette haute situation, à cette situation de bouée, de borne?

Par son mérite, son mérite agricole et personnel. Je dis 'agricole', parce qu'il cultive l'amour du jeste et du Beau. Nous arrivons à un point délicat. Les critiques sont recrutés au choix, comme les produits dits de choix, extra-supérieurs, de première qualité.

C'est le Directeur d'un journal, d'une revue, ou de tout autre périodique, qui découvre le critique nécessaire à la bonne composition de sa rédaction. AUCUNE RECOMMENDATION NE PEUT AGIR. Il le découvre à la suite d'un sévère examen, d'un examen de conscience. Cet examen est très long et très pénible, aussi bien pour le critique que pour le Directeur. L'un, interoge, l'autre, se méfie. C'est une lutte angoissante, pleine d'inattendu. Toutes les ruses sont employées de part et d'autre. Enfin le Directeur est vaincu. C'est ce qui arrive ordinairement si le critique est de bonne race, et si son entraînement a été soigneusement conçu. Le Directeur est absorbé, résorbé par le critique.

Il est rare que le Directeur en réchappe.

* * *

Le vrai sens critique ne consiste pas à se critiquer soi-même, mais à critiquer les autres; et la poutre que l'on a dans l'œil, n'empèche nullement de voir la paille qui est dans celui de son voisin: dans ce cas, la poutre devient une longue-vue, très longue, qui grossit la paille d'une façon démesurée.

On ne saurait trop admirer le courage du premier critique qui se présenta dans le monde. Les gens grossiers de la Vieille Nuit des Temps durent le recevoir à grands coups de souliers dans le ventre, ne se rendant point compte qu'il était un précurseur; digne de vénération. A sa manière, ce fut un héros.

Les deuxième, troisième, quatrième et cinquième critiques ne furent certainement pas mieux reçus . . . mais aidèrent à créer un précédent. L'Art critique se donnait le jour à lui-même. Ce fut son premier jour de l'an. Longtemps après, ces Bienfaiteurs de l'Humanité, surent mieux s'organiser; ils fondèrent des syndicats de la critique dans toutes les grandes capitales. Les critiques devinrent ainsi des personnages considérables, ce qui prouve que la vertu est toujours récompensée. Du coup, les artistes étaient bridés, soumis comme des chats-tigres. Il est juste que les Artistes soient guidés par les critiques. Je n'ai jamais compris la susceptibilité des artistes devant les avertissements des critiques. Je crois qu'il y a là de l'orgueil, un orgueil mal placé, qui déplaît. Les artistes gagneraient à mieux vénérer les critiques; à les écouter respectueusement; à les aimer même; à les inviter souvent à la table de famille, entre l'oncle et le grand-père. Qu'ils suivent mon exemple, mon bon exemple, je suis ébloui par la présence d'un critique, son éclat est tel, que je cligne des yeux pendant plus d'une heure; je baise la trace de ses pantoufles; je bois ses paroles dans un grand verre à pied, par politesse. J'ai beaucoup étudié les moeurs des animaux. Hélas! ils n'ont pas de critiques. Cet art leur est étranger; du moins je ne connais aucun ouvrage de ce genre dans les archives de mes animaux. Peut-être, mes amis critiques en connaissent-ils un ou plusieurs. Qu'ils soient assez gentils pour le dire, le plus tôt possible serait le mieux. Oui, les animaux n'ont pas de critiques. Le loup ne critique pas le mouton: il le mange; non pas qu'il méprise l'art du mouton, mais parce qu'il admire la chair, et même les os du laineux animal, si bon, si bon, en ragoût.

Il nous faut une discipline de fer, ou de tout autre métal. Seuls les critiques peuvent l'imposer, la faire observer, de loin. Ils ne demandent qu'à nous inculquer les excellents principes de l'obéissance. Celui qui désobéit est bien à plaindre, ne pas obéir est bien triste. Mais il ne faut pas obéir à ses mauvaises passions, même si elles nous en donnent l'ordre elles-mêmes. A quoi reconnaît-on que des passions sont mauvaises, mauvaises comme la gale? Oui, à quoi?

Au plaisir que l'on prend à s'y abandonner, à s'y livrer, ET QU'ELLES DÉPLAISENT AUX CRITIQUES.

Eux n'ont pas de mauvaises passions. Comment en auraient-ils, les braves gens? Ils n'ont pas de passions du tout, *aucune*. Toujours calmes, ils ne songent qu'à leur devoir, corriger les défauts du pauvre monde, et s'en faire un revenu convenable, pour s'acheter du tabac, tout simplement.

C'est là leur tâche; cette tâche incombe à des hommes de bons conseils, parce qu'ils en ont mille pour un, des conseils, des conseils régionaux.

* * *

Remercions les de tous les sacrifices qu'ils font journellement pour notre bien, pour notre seul bien, demandons à la Providence de les protéger contre les maladies de toutes sortes, de les éloigner des ennuis de tous genres; de leur accorder un grand nombre d'enfants de toute espèce, qui continuent la leur. Ces souhaits ne peuvent leur faire ni bien ni mal. En tous cas, cela leur fera une belle jambe . . . pour écrire.

ERIK SATIE.

Extrait de *Action* No. 8 — août 1921.

3

MÉMOIRES D'UN AMNÉSIQUE (fragment)
RECOINS DE MA VIE

L'origine des Satie remonte, peut-être, aux temps les plus reculés. Oui . . . Là-dessus, je ne puis rien affirmer — ni infirmer, du reste . . .

Cependant, je suppose que cette famille n'appartenait pas à la Noblesse (*même du Pape*) ; que ses membres étaient de bons et modestes corvéables à merci, ce qui, autrefois, était un honneur et un plaisir (*pour le bon seigneur du corvéable, bien entendu*). Oui . . .

Ce que firent les Satie lors de la Guerre de Cent ans, je l'ignore ; je n'ai, non plus, aucun renseignement sur leur attitude et sur la part qu'ils prirent à celle de Trente ans (*une de nos plus belles guerres*).

Que la mémoire de mes vieux ascendants repose en paix. Oui . . .

Passons. Je reviendra sur ce sujet.

* * *

Pour ce qui est de moi, je suis né à Honfleur (Calvados), arrondissement de Pont-l'Evêque, le 17 mai 1866 . . . Me voici donc quinquagénaire, ce qui est un titre comme un autre.

Honfleur est une petite ville qu'arrosent ensemble — et de connivence — les flots poétiques de la Seine et ceux tumultueux de la Manche. Ses habitants (honfleurais) sont très polis et très aimables. Oui . . .

Je restai dans cette cité jusqu'à l'âge de douze ans (1878) et vins me fixer à Paris . . . J'eus une enfance et une adolescence quelconques — sans traits dignes d'être relatés dans de sérieux écrits. Aussi, n'en parlerai-je pas.

Passons. Je reviendrai sur ce sujet.

* * *

Je grille d'envie de vous donner, ici, mon signalement (*énumération de mes particularités physiques — celles dont je puis honnêtement parler évidemment*) : . . . Cheveux et sourcils châtain foncé; yeux gris (*pommelés, probablement*); front couvert; nez long; bouche moyenne; menton large; visage ovale. Taille: 1 mètre 67 centimètres.

Ce document signalétique date de 1887, époque où je fis mon volontariat au 33e régiment d'infanterie à Arras (Pas-de-Calais). Il ne pourrait me servir aujourd'hui.

Je regrette de ne pas vous montrer mes empreintes digitales (*de doigt*). Oui. Je ne les ai pas sur moi, et ces reproductions spéciales ne sont pas belles à voir (*elles ressemblent à Vuillermoz et à Laloy réunis*).

Passons. Je reviendrai sur ce sujet.

140

Après une assez courte adolescence, je devins un jeune homme ordinairement potable, pas plus. C'est à ce moment de ma vie que je commençai à penser et à écrire musicalement. Oui.

Fâcheuse idée! . . . très fâcheuse idée! . . .

En effet, car je ne tardai pas à faire usage d'une originalité (*originale*) déplaisante, hors de propos, anti-française, contre-nature, etc. . . .

Alors, la vie fut pour moi tellement intenable, que je résolus de me retirer dans mes terres et de passer mes jours dans une tour d'ivoire — ou d'un autre métal (*métallique*).

C'est ainsi que je pris goût pour la misanthropie; que je cultivai l'hypocondrie; et que je fus le plus mélancolique (*de plomb*) des humains. Je faisais peine à voir — même avec un lorgnon en or contrôlé. Oui.

Et tout cela m'est advenu par la faute de la Musique. Cet art m'a fait plus de mal que de bien, lui: il m'a brouillé avec nombre de gens de qualité, fort honorables, plus que distingués, très 'comme il faut'.

Passons. Je reviendrai sur ce sujet.

* * *

Personnellement, je ne suis ni bon ni mauvais. J'oscille, puis-je dire. Aussi, n'ai-je jamais fait réellement de mal à quiconque — ni de bien, au surplus.

Toutefois, j'ai beaucoup d'ennemis — de fidèles ennemis, naturellement. Pourquoi? Cela tient à ce que, pour la plupart, ils ne me connaissent pas — ou ne me connaissent que de seconde main, par ouï-dire (*des mensonges plus que menteurs*), en somme.

L'homme ne peut être parfait. Je ne leur en veux nullement: ils sont les premières victimes de leur inconscience et de leur manque de perspicacité . . . Pauvres gens! . . .

Aussi, les plains-je.

Passons. Je reviendrai sur ce sujet.

ERIK SATIE.

Feuilles Libres, 5ème Année, No. 35,
janvier-février 1924.

4
MÉMOIRES D'UN AMNÉSIQUE
CE QUE JE SUIS (Fragment)

Toute le monde vous dira que je ne suis pas un musicien.[1] C'est juste.

Dès le début de ma carrière, je me suis, de suite, classé parmi les phonométrographes. Mes travaux sont de la pure phonométrique. Que l'on prenne le *Fils des Etoiles* ou les *Morceaux en forme de poire*, *En habit de Cheval* ou les *Sarabandes*, on perçoit qu'aucune idée musicale n'a présidé à la création de ces œuvres. C'est la pensée scientifique qui domine.

Du reste, j'ai plus de plaisir à mesurer un son que je n'en ai à l'entendre. Le phénomètre à la main, je travaille joyeusement et sûrement.

Que n'ai-je pesé ou mesuré? Tout de Beethoven, tout de Verdi, etc. C'est très curieux.

La première fois que je me servis d'un phonoscope, j'examinai un si bémol de moyenne grosseur. Je n'ai, je vous assure, jamais vu chose plus répugnante.   J'appelai mon domestique pour le lui faire voir.

Au phono-peseur un fa dièse ordinaire, très commun, atteignit 93 kilogrammes. Il émanait d'un fort gros ténor dont je pris le poids.

Connaissez-vous le nettoyage des sons? C'est assez sale. Le filage est plus propre; savoir les classer est très minutieux et demande une bonne vue. Ici nous sommes dans la phonotechnique.

Quant aux explosions sonores, souvent si désagréables, le coton, fixé dans les oreilles, les atténue, poir soi, convenablement. Ici, nous sommes dans la pyrophonie.

Pour écrire mes *Pièces Froides*, je me suis servi d'un caléidophone-enregistreur. Cela prit sept minutes. J'appelai mon domestique pour les lui faire entendre.

Je crois pouvoir dire que la phonologie est supérieure à la musique. C'est plus varié. Le rendement pécuniaire est plus grand. Je lui dois ma fortune.

En tous cas, au motodynamophone, un phonométreur médiocrement exercé peut, facilement, noter plus de sons que ne le fera le plus habile musicien, dans le même temps, avec le même effort. C'est grâce à cela que j'ai tant ecrit.

L'avenir est donc à la philophonie.

ERIK SATIE.

1. Voir : O. Séré, *Musiciens français d'aujourd'hui*, p.138.

S.I.M., 15.4.1912.

5
MÉMOIRES D'UN AMNÉSIQUE
L'INTELLIGENCE ET LA MUSICALITÉ
CHEZ LES ANIMAUX

L'intelligence des animaux est au-dessus de toute négation. Mais que fait l'homme pour améliorer l'état mental de ces concitoyens résignés? Il leur offre une instruction médiocre, espacée, incomplète, telle qu'un enfant n'en voudrait pas pour lui-même; et il aurait raison, le cher petit être. Cette instruction consiste surtout à développer l'instinct de cruauté et de vice qui existe ataviquement chez les individus. Il n'est jamais question, dans les programmes de cet enseignement, ni d'art, ni de littérature, ni de sciences naturelles, morales, ou d'autres matières. Les pigeons voyageurs ne sont nullement préparés à leur mission par un usage de la géographie; les poissons sont tenus à l'écart de l'étude de l'océanographie; les bœufs, les moutons, les veaux ignorent tout de l'agencement raisonné d'un abattoir moderne, et ne savent pas quel est leur rôle nutritif dans la société que s'est constituée l'homme.

Peu d'animaux bénéficient de l'instruction humaine. Le chien, le mulet, le cheval, l'âne, le perroquet, le merle et quelques autres, sont les seuls animaux qui reçoivent un semblant d'instruction. Encore, est-ce plutôt de l'éducation qu'autre chose. Comparez, je vous prie, cette instruction à celle donnée par les universités à un jeune bachelier humain, et vous voyez qu'elle est nulle et qu'elle ne peut étendre ni faciliter les connaissances que l'animal aura pu acquérir par ses travaux, par son assiduité à ceux-ci. Mais, musicalement? Des chevaux ont appris à danser; des araignées se sont tenues sous un piano pendant toute la durée d'un long concert, concert organisé pour elles par un maître respecté du clavier. Et après? Rien. Par-ci, par-là, on nous entretient de la musicalité du sansonnet, de la mémoire mélodique du corbeau, de l'ingéniosité harmonique du hibou qui s'accompagne en se tapant sur le ventre, moyen purement artificiel et de mince polyphonie.

Quant au rossignol, toujours cité, son savoir musical fait hausser les épaules au plus ignorant de ses auditeurs. Non seulement sa voix n'est pas posée, mais il n'a aucune connaissance ni des clefs, ni de la tonalité, ni de la modalité, ni de la mesure. Peut-être est il doué? C'est possible; c'est même certain. Mais on peut affirmer que sa culture artistique n'égale pas ses dons naturels, et que cette voix, dont il se montre si orgueilleux, n'est qu'un instrument très inférieur et inutile en soi.

(A suivre)

ERIK SATIE

S.I.M. 1er février 1914.

Appendix D

LIST OF PUBLISHED WORKS BY ERIK SATIE

S. = Editions Salabert (formerly Rouart, Lerolle & Cie.). E. = Editions Eschig.
U. = Editions Universal. o.p. = Out of Print.

PIANO SOLO	Publisher	Date
Ogives	o.p.	1886
3 Sarabandes	S.	1887
3 Gymnopédies	S.	1888
3 Gnossiennes	S.	1890
3 Préludes from Le Fils des Étoiles	S.	1891
Sonneries de la Rose Croix	S.	1892
Danses Gothiques	S. (posth.)	1893
4 Préludes: Fête en l'honneur d'une jeune demoiselle; Prélude d'Eginhard; 1ère Prélude du Nazaréen; 2me Prélude du Nazaréen	S. (posth.)	1893
Prélude de la Porte Héroique du Ciel	S.	1894
Messe des Pauvres (organ or piano)	S. (posth.)	1895
Pièces Froides (Airs à faire fuir and Danses de travers)	S.	1897
Prélude en Tapisserie	S. (posth.)	1906
Passacaille	S. (posth.)	1906
3 Préludes Flasques (pour un chien)	E.	1912
Descriptions Automatiques	E.	1913
Embryons Desséchés	E.	1913
Croquis et Agaceries d'un Gros Bonhomme en Bois	E.	1913
Chapitres tournés en tous Sens	E.	1913
Enfantines: (1) Menus Propos Enfantins; (2) Enfantillages Pittoresques; (3) Peccadilles Importunes	E.	1913
Vieux Séquins et Vieilles Cuirasses	E.	1914
Heures Séculaires et Instantanées	E.	1914
Trois Valses du Précieux Degoûté	S.	1914
Sports et Divertissements	S.	1914
Les Pantins Dansent	S. (posth.)	1914
Avant-Dernières Pensées	S.	1915
Sonatine Bureaucratique	S.	1917
5 Nocturnes	S.	1919
Menuet	E.	1920
Relâche (arr. from Ballet)	S.	1924
Mercure (arr. from Ballet)	U.	1924

There are also Piano arrangements of the following Music-Hall and Café Songs and Dances:

Je te Veux (Waltz)	S.
Le Piccadilly	S.
Poudre d'Or	S.
Rag-time Parade	S.
La Diva de l'Empire	S.

PIANO DUET (Four Hands)	Publisher	Date
3 Morceaux en Forme de Poire	S.	1903
Aperçus Désagréables	E.	1908
En Habit de Cheval (Exists also for Orch.)	S.	1911
Parade (Ballet Suite, arr. by composer)	S.	1917
Cinéma (Entracte symphonique, arr. from Ballet Relâche by Milhaud)	S.	1924
Trois Petites Pièces Montées (arr. from Orch.)	E.	1920

PIANO and VIOLIN

Choses Vues à Droite et à Gauche (sans lunettes)	S.	1912

SONGS—Voice and Piano

Trois Poèmes d'Amour	S.	1914
Trois Mélodies: Daphénéo, La Statue de Bronze, Le Chapelier	S.	1916
Quatre Petites Mélodies	E.	1920
Ludions	S.	1923

(Popular)

Je te Veux; Tendrement; La Diva de l'Empire	S.	

VOICE and ORCHESTRA

Socrate ('Drame symphonique' in three parts for four voices and orchestra)	E.	1919

STAGE WORKS

Incidental music to Le Fils des Étoiles (Jules Bois), Orch. flutes and harps only. Prelude to 1st Act re-orchestrated by Ravel in 1913. (3 Preludes)	S.	1891
Geneviève de Brabant (miniature opera for marionettes)	U.	1899
Jack-in-the-Box (written for pantomime, never performed. Original piano score orch. in 1929 by Milhaud)	U.	1899
Le Piège de Méduse (Comedy with music)	o.p.	1913
Ed. De Luxe, with illustrations by Brague, Galerie Simon, Paris, 1921.		
5 Grimaces (for Cocteau's unrealised production of Midsummer Night's Dream)	o.p.	1914

BALLETS

Uspud (privately printed)	o.p.	1892
Parade (Ballet Réaliste)	S.	1917
Mercure (Poses Plastiques)	U.	1924
Relâche (Ballet Instantanéiste)	S.	1924

ORCHESTRAL

3 Petites Pièces Montées (small orch.)	E.	1919
La Belle Excentrique (music-hall orch.)	E.	1920
En Habit de Cheval	S.	1911

(Popular)

Le Piccadilly, March (small orch.)	S.	
Je te Veux, Waltz (small orch.)	S.	
La Diva de l'Empire (small orch.)	S.	
Rag-Time Parade (small orch.)	S.	

ORCHESTRAL ARRANGEMENTS

Gymnopédies (First and Third), arr. Debussy	S.	
Jack-in-the-Box, arr. Milhaud	U.	
Gnossienne (No. 3), arr. Poulenc	M.S.	

146

Index

Académie des Beaux Arts, 30, 31
Action, 114, 136–139
Adamson, H., *The Muses' Threnodie*, 21n.
Allais, Alphonse, 15
Andersen, Hans, 17
Ansermet, Ernest, 102
Anton, Jane Leslie (Jane Satie), 14
Aragon, Louis, 62, 106
Arcueil-Cachan, Satie at, 36, 37, 38, 48, 49, 66, 100, 123, 124; "Bon Maitre d'," 108, 124; "Ecole d'," 65, 66; "Soviet d'," 112
Arp, Hans, 62
Arras, military service at, 18, 140
Auberge du Clou, 31, 34
Auric, Georges, 19, 41, 51, 53, 127
Auriol, Georges, *The Velvet Gentleman*, 125 n.

Bach, 51, 93
Barnetsche, Eugénie, 16
Bartók, 90
Bathori, Jane, 55
Baudelaire, *Poèmes*, 33
Beaumont, Count Étienne de, 61
Beethoven, 54, 67, 119, 121, 142
Belgium, lecture tour in, 65
Bertin, Pierre, 47, 60, 62
Bibliothèque Nationale, 18, 112
Bizet, 105
Bois, Jules, 29, 145
Borlin, Jean, 63, 106
Braque, 41, 116
Breton, André, 62, 106
Bruneau, Alfred, *Le Rêve*, 19
Brussel, Robert, 110

Calvocoressi, M.-D., 42, 110
Carroll, Lewis, 46, 47; *Alice in Wonderland*, 82, 95
Cartulaire de l'Eglise Métropolitaine d'Art de Jésus Conducteur, Le, 10, 25, 27–28, 120, 131–2
Caryathis, Mlle., 59
Cercle Musical, 43
Cézanne, 32, 116
Chabrier, Emmanuel, *Le Roi Malgré Lui*, 68 (illus.), 79, 105, 116, 117, 129
Chagall, 101
Chaldæan Confraternity, 23. See Rose + Croix
Chalupt, René, 95
Chaplin, Charlie, 103
Charpentier, Gustave, 31
Chat Noir Cabaret, 22, 31
Châtelet Theatre, 49, 52, 102
Chausson, 116
Chavannes, Puvis de, 23, 32, 71
Chirico, 101
Chopin, 54, 92; *Funeral March*, 44, 79
Cigale Theatre, La, 61, 105
Clair, René, 63, 106
Clementi, 90
Cliquet-Pleyel, Henri, 65, 66
Cocteau, Jean, 32, 36 and n., 39, 41, 44, 48, 49, 50 and n., 51, 52, 53, 54, 57, 66, 95, 96, 102 and n., 104–5, 108, 113, 124, 127, 128; *Le Coq* broadsheets, 53, 54; *Le Coq et l'Arlequin*, 36 and n., 50 and n., 53, 102 and n.; *Danseuse*, 96; adaptation of *Midsummer Night's Dream*, 49, 145; *Parade*, 49–53, 102–5
Cœur, Le, 29–30
Colette, 27

Collet, Henri, 52
Comédie Parisienne, 100
Conservatoire, 16, 30, 40, 54, 75, 111, 116
Contamine de Latour, J. P., 17, 18, 24, 34, 99, 100, 131
Coq, Le, Broadsheets, 53, 54
Cortot, Alfred, 44, 45 and n., 46, 57, 67, 82, 85
Couperin, 45
Cousin, Victor, 54, 57, 96
Cubism, 49, 50, 63, 104

Dadaism, 47, 62, 63, 101, 107, 128
Danse Macabre, 60
Darty, Paulette, 38, 39, 108
Debussy, Claude, 5 (Introduction), 19, 23, 30, 31, 32, 33, 34, 39, 40, 41, 42, 43, 44, 48, 49, 52, 54, 58 and n., 59–60, 68, 75, 79, 85, 93, 95, 96, 117, 126, 127, 128, 129; *Prélude à l'Après-midi d'un Faune*, 68; *String Quartet*, 68; *Jardins sous la Pluie*, 80; *Children's Corner*, 80, 90; *Pelléas*, 32, 99, 128; orchestrates *Gymnopédies*, 19, 42, 71 and n.; Satie's lecture on, 32; relations with Satie, 31–34, 42–43, 48, 52, 54, 58, 95; *Elégie*, dedicated to, 59, 95
Debussy, Mme, 79, 80
Delgrange, M., 60
Demets, publishers, 43, 78
Depaquit, 100
Derain, 100, 108, 116
Désormière, Roger, 65
Diaghilev, Serge de, 49, 50, 100, 102, 105. See Russian Ballet
Dubois, M., 31
Duchamp, Marcel, *Relâche*, 63
Dukas, Paul, 85, 117
Durand, publisher, 49, 78
Durey, Louis, 53

Ecorcheville, J., 43n., 110
Eglise Métropolitaine d'Art de Jésus Conducteur, L', 25
Eluard, Paul, 62
Ernst, Max, 62, 106
Esprit Nouveau, 116n.

Fargue, Leon-Paul, 94, 96
Fauré, Gabriel, 16, 68, 74
Féraudy, Maurice de, *Pousse l'Amour*, 101
Feuilles Libres, Les, 58n., 116n., 117n., 118, 130 n., 140–141
Field, John, 92
Flaubert, 18, *La Tentation de Saint Antoine*, 35; *Salammbô*, 71
Franck, César, 40, 116, 127
Frueh, 123

Galérie Barbazanges, 60
Galérie Durand-Ruel, 22
Gauthier-Villars, M., 25, 27–8, 114, 131, 132
Gebrauchsmusik, 56
Gil Blas, letter to, 24–25, 131
Godebski, M., 94
Gounod, 30, 31, 67, 80, 93, 95
"Grant-Plumot, Sir William," dedication to, 80
Guichard, Leon, 94n.
Guilmant, Félix, 16, 54
Guiraud, Ernest, 30, 31

Haydn, 113

Herodotus, 71n.
Honegger, Arthur, 41, 53
Honfleur, 13, 14, 15, 16, 110, 140, Collège d', 13, 14
Hôpital St. Joseph, 66
Hugo, Victor, 27, 132
Hyspa, Vincent, 38

Impressionism and Impressionists, 39, 44, 50, 54, 128
Indy, Vincent d', 40, 41, 42, 54, 77, 116
Institut de France, 30, 31

Jacob, Max, 60
Jacob, Maxime, 65, 66

Kipling, Rudyard, *Cat that Walked by Himself*, 128
Koechlin, Charles, 19, 41, 57, 73, 85, 90, 93, 128

La Bruyère, *Characters*, 83
Lalo, 116
Laloy, Louis, 33, 116, 140
Lamartine, 95
Lambert, Constant, *Music Ho!*, 51 and n., 106 and n.
Lavignac, *Music and Musicians*, 116, 117
Leacock, Stephen, 119n.
Lear, Edward, 47, 78, 82
Lenepveu, M., 31
Liszt, 54
Lopokova, 102
Louis XI, dedication to, 80
Lugné-Poë, 25

Maeterlinck, 32, 128, *Princesse Maleine*, 32, *Pelléas et Mélisande*, 32
Manet, 116
Maritain, Jacques, 28
Marnold, Jean, 57, 99, 114
Martin, Charles, 45, 87
Mascotte, La, 79
Massenet, 67, 93
Massine, 50, 61, 102, 105
Mathias, 16
Matisse, 60
Mellers, W. H., *Studies in Contemporary Music*, 22n., 56n., 126n.
Mendès, Catulle, *Rodrigue et Chimène*, 128
Ménéstrel, Le, 30
Mercure de France, 99, 114
Mignon, 60
Milhaud, Darius, 19, 39, 41, 45, 53, 60, *La Création du Monde*, 63, 66, 85, 100, 108, 113, 129
Mill, John Stuart, 29
Monet, Claude, 32
Monte Carlo, 101
Montmartre, 22, 25, 34, 36, 37, 38, 39, 48, 59, 61, 124
Montparnasse, 48
Mozart, 54, 79, 113
Musique d'ameublement, 59, 60, 96
Musique de Familles, 17
Mussorgsky, 32, 54

Niedermeyer, 15
Nouveaux Jeunes, Les, 52, and see *Les Six*
Notre Dame, 18, 64

Opéra, Paris, 34, 35, 99–100

Paladilhe, M., 31
Pascal, 30
Péladan, Joseph ("Sâr"), 18, 21, 22, 24, 25, 30, 131; *Le Fils des Etoiles*, 22, 23, 32, 72; *Prince de Byzance*, 29
Picabia, Francis, *Relâche*, 63, 64, 65, 106, 107

Picasso, 41, 49, 54, 63, 116; and *Para e*, 50, 51, 52, 102, 105; and *Mercure*, 61, 62, 105, 106
Plainsong, 16, 18, 22, 28, 94
Plato, *Dialogues*, 54, 56, 57, 69, 96, 97; and see *Socrate*
Polignac, Princesse de, 54, 55, 96
Poulenc, 41, 53, 106, 129
Prix de Rome, 19, 32, 116

Rabelais, 59
Radiguet, Raymond, 17, 95, *Adieu*, 96; 108
Ravel, Maurice, 5 (Introduction), 19 and n. 41, 42, 48, 53, 58, 93, 110, 127; *Ma Mère l'Oye*, 129
Rembrandt, 121
Revue Musicale, La, 45n., 59, 67, 94n., 125n.
Rimbaud, 51
Rimsky-Korsakov, 54
Rip, 80
Rodin, 114, 136
Roland-Manuel, M., 43 and n., 72, 77, 78, 80, 87, 110 and n., 122 and n. See also Satie's *Letters*
Rome, 49, 50; and see Prix de Rome
Rose+Croix, 18, 21 and n., 22, 23, 24, 25, 29, 30, 36, 55, 72, 100
Rosicrucianism; see Rose+Croix
Rossini, *Péchés de ma Vieillesse*, 45n.; *La Boutique Fantasque*, 45n.
Rouart-Lerolle, publishers, 43, 144
Rousseau, Le Douanier, 112
Roussel, 41, 77, 85, 116 and n.
Russian Ballet, 39, 52, 102. See also Diaghilev.

St. Catherine, Church of, 14, 15
Saint-Saëns, 30, 116
Sainte-Beuve, 30
Salis, Rudolf, 22, 31
Salle Pleyel, 110
Satie, Adrien, "Seabird," 13, 14, 15, 16, 47, 125
Satie, Alfred, 13, 16, 17, 93
Satie, Captain, 13
Satie, Conrad, 14, 19, 29–30, 34, 41. See Satie's *Letters*
Satie, Erik Alfred Leslie, Birth, parentage, 14; military service, 18, 35; death, 55, 66
Satie, Erik, Letters to: Cocteau, Jean, 32; Debussy, 33–34; Gauthier-Villars, M. (in *Le Cartulaire*), 27–28, 131–132; *Gil Blas*, 24–25, 131; Roland-Manuel, M., 43n., 49n., 77, 78, 80; Saint-Saëns, M. (in *Le Ménéstrel*), 30; Satie, Conrad, 19, 41–2; Unnamed, 123, 124
Satie, Erik, Works of (including projected works):
Adieu, see *Petites Mélodies, Quatre*
Affolements Granitiques, illus, 81, 82; and see *Heures Séculaires*
Airs à faire fuir, see *Pièces Froides*
Anges, Les, 17, 93
Aperçus Désagréables, 42 and n., 77, 111
Aubade, see *Avant-Dernières Pensées*
Avant-Dernières Pensées, 85
Bain de Mer, see *Sports et Divertissements*
Balançoire, La, see *Sports et Divertissements*; illus., 91
Bâtard de Tristan, Le, 34
Belle, Excentrique, La, 59
Carnaval, Le, see *Sports et Divertissements*
Celle qui Parle Trop, see *Chapitres tournés en tous sens*
Chapelier, Le, see *Mélodies, Trois*
Chapitres tournés en tous Sens, 69, 79–80, 111
Chasse, La, see *Sports et Divertissements*
Choral, 87, illus. 89, and see *Sports et Divertissements*
Choses Vues à Droite et à Gauche (sans lunettes), 93

Index

Coco-Chéri, see *Pousse l'Amour*, 101
Colin-Maillard, see *Sports et Divertissements*
Comédie Italienne, see *Sports et Divertissements*
Corcleru, 35
Courses, Les, see *Sports et Divertissements*
Crépuscule matinal (de midi), see *Heures Séculaires*
Croquis et Agaceries d'un Gros Bonhomme en Bois, 69, 79, 111
Danse maigre (à la manière de ces messieurs), see *Croquis et Agaceries*
Danses de Travers, 43, and see *Pièces Froides*
Danses Gothiques, 29, 75, 94
Danseuse, see *Petites Melodies, Quatre*
Daphénéo, see *Melodies, Trois*
Descriptions Automatiques, 78, 111
Diva de l'Empire, La, 39, 144
Edriophthalma, see *Embryons Desséchés*
Elégie, see *Petites Mélodies, Quatre*
Embryons Desséchés, 44, 69, 78–9, 111
En Habit de Cheval, 43, 77, 119, 142
Enfantillages Pittoresques, 15n., 69, 80, and see *Enfantines*
Entr'acte Cinématographique, 60, 61, 63, 108, and see *Relâche*
Españana, see *Croquis et Agaceries*
Fantaisie-Valse, 17
Fête en l'honneur d'une jeune demoiselle, see *Préludes*, 4
Feu d'artifice, see *Sports et Divertissements*
Fils des Etoiles, Le (3 *Préludes*), 22, 23, 32, 42, 68, 72, 75, 110, 142
Fleurs, Les, 17, 93
Flirt, see *Sports et Divertissements*
Geneviève de Brabant, 47, 100
Gnossiennes, 3, 36, 39, 43, 69, 71–2, illus., 72, 73, 94, 127, 143
Golf, Le, see *Sports et Divertissements*
Grimaces, 5, 49
Gymnopédies, 3, 5, 18–19, 29, 30, 32, 36, 39, 42, 43, 55, 64, 65, 68–69; illus. 69, 70 and 71; 71 and n., 74, 82, 84, 92, 127, 129, illus. 129
Heures Séculaires et Instantanées, 45, 69, 80–82, illus. 81, 82, 128
Holothurie, see *Embryons Desséchés*
Hymne au Drapeau, 29
Idylle, see *Avant-Dernières Pensées*
Irnebizolle, 35
Jack in the Box, 39, 100
Je te Veux, 38, 39, 143
Ludions, 96, 145
Marche du Grand Escalier, 15, and see *Enfantillages Pittoresques*
Mariée, La, see *Sports et Divertissements*
Méditation, see *Avant-Dernières Pensées*
Mélodies, Trois, 55, 94–5
Menuet, 92, 144
Menus Propos Enfantins, 80, and see *Enfantines*
Mercure, 61, 63, 101, 105–6
Messe des Pauvres, 29–30, 72, 94
Morceaux en Forme de Poire, 3, 39–40, 49, 75, illus. 76, 102, 119, 142
Naissance de Venus, 108
Ne suis que grain de Sable, see *Poèmes d'Amour*
Neuvanines pour le plus grand calme et la forte tranquillité de mon âme, mises sous l'invocation de Saint Benoît, 29
Nocturnes, 5, 59, 90, 92, illus. 92, 108, 127
Obstacles Vénimeux, see *Heures Séculaires*
Ogives, 18, 94
On joue, see *Véritables Preludes Flasques*
Ontrotance, 35
Pantins Dansent, Les, 75
Parade, 5 (Introduction), 19, 39, 49–52, 54, 59, 61, 62, 63, 101, 102–105, illus. 103; 108, 127, 128
Passacaille, 77

Paul et Virginie, 108
Peccadilles Importunes, 80, and see *Enfantine*
Pêche, La, see *Sports et Divertissements*
Petites Mélodies, Quatre, 59, 95–6, illus. 95
Petites Pièces Montées, Trois, 59
Pièces Froides, 35, 36, 73–4, illus. 74, 120, 127, 142
Pièces Montées, see *Petites Pièces Montées*
Piège de Méduse, Le, 47, 62, 63, 101–2, 122, 128
Pieuvre, Le, see *Sports et Divertissements*, illus. 86
Pique-Nique, see *Sports et Divertissements*
Podophthalma, see *Embryons Desséchés*
Poèmes d'Amour, Trois, 23n., 94, illus. 94
Porteur de grosses pierres, Le, see *Chapitres tournés en tous sens*
Poudre d'Or, 39
Pousse l'Amour, 47, 100–1
Préludes, 4, 29, 75, 94
Prélude d'Eginhard, see *Préludes*, 4
Prélude de la Porte Héroïque du Ciel, 23, 29, 43, 68, 72, illus. 73
Prélude du Nazaréen, 1ère, see *Préludes*, 4
Prélude du Nazaréen, 2me, see *Préludes*, 4
Prélude en Tapisserie, 75
Préludes Flasques (pour un chien), 3, see *Véritables Preludes Flasques*
Princesse Maleine, 32, 128
Quatre Coins, Les, see *Sports et Divertissements*
Regrets des Enfermés, see *Chapitres tournés en tous sens*
Relâche, 60, 61, 63–65, 101, 106–108, illus. 107
Sa Taille, see *Valses, Distinguées, du Précieux Dégoûté*
Sarabandes, 19, illus. 20; 29, 42, 65, 67, 68, illus. 68; 69, 119, 127, 142
Ses Jambes, see *Valses Distinguées du Précieux Dégoûté*
Seul à la masion, see *Véritables Préludes Flasques*
Sévère Réprimande, see *Véritables Préludes Flasques*
Socrate, 5 (Introduction), 35, 53, 55–58, 59, 60, 64, 69, 87, 92, 96–99; illus. 97 and n. and 98; 108, 127, 128
Son Binocle, see *Valses Distinguées du Précieux Dégoûté*
Sonatine Bureaucratique, 45, 90
Sonneries de la Rose Croix, 22, 23, 71
Sports et Divertissements, 45, 85, illus. 86; 87–90, illus. 89, 91; 127
Statue de Bronze, La, see *Mélodies, Trois*
Suis chauve de naissance, see *Poèmes d'Amour*
Sur la Lanterne, see *Descriptions Automatiques*
Sur un Vaisseau, see *Descriptions Automatiques*
Sylvie, 17, 93
Ta parure est secrète, see *Poèmes d'Amour*
Tango, Le, see *Sports et Divertissements*
Tendrement, 38
Tennis, Le, see *Sports et Divertissements*
Traineau, see *Sports et Divertissements*
Tumisrudebude, 35
Tyrolienne Turque, see *Croquis et Agaceries*
Uspud, 34–35, illus. facing p. 100, 99–100, 133–4
Valse-Ballet, 17
Valses Distinguées du Précieux Dégoûté, Trois, 45, 82–84, illus. 84 and 85
Véritables Préludes Flasques, 3, 43, 77–8, 110, 111, 128
Vieux Sequins et Vieilles Cuirasses, 45, 80, 111
Water Chute, see *Sports et Divertissements*
Yachting, see *Sports et Divertissements*
Satie, Erik
Writings:
Article in *Les Feuilles Libres*, June-July, 1922, quoted 116–7

Index

Article in *Les Feuilles Libres*, March, 1923, quoted, 130
Cahiers d'un Mammifère (*Esprit Nouveau*, April, 1921), 116 and n.
Cartulaire de l'Eglise Metropolitaine d'Art de Jésus Conducteur, Le, 10, 25, quoted 27–28; 120
Cœur, Le, 29
Coq, Le, Broadsheets, 53, 54
Eloge des Critiques (*Action*, August, 1921), 114n., quoted 114–5; 120, French text, 136–139
Journalism at Arcueil, quoted 38
Mémoires d'un Amnésique, 118–123:
  Mes Trois Candidatures (S.I.M., Nov. 1912), 31 and n.
  Day in the Life of a Musician (S.I.M., Feb., 1913), quoted 46–7; 118; French text, 135
  Ce que Je Suis (S.I.M., April, 1912), quoted 119–120; 120n. French text 142
  Recoins de ma Vie (*Les Feuilles Libres*, Jan.-Feb., 1924), quoted 118–9; French text, 140–141
  Parfait Entourage, quoted, 121–2
  Choses de Théâtre, quoted 122–3
  Intelligence and Musical Appreciation among Animals (S.I.M., Feb., 1914), 114 and n., quoted 120–121, French text, 146

Périmés, Les (*Les Feuilles Libres*, March, 1923), 58n.
Piège de Méduse, Le, 101–102, and see Works
Poèmes d'Amour, Trois, 94
Preface to *Heures Séculaires*, 45
Preface to *Sports et Divertissements*, 87
Self-portrait for publisher's catalogue, 110–111
Shadow Play (M.S.), 122
Stravinsky, Propos à Propos de Igor (*Les Feuilles Libres*, Oct.-Nov., 1922), 117

Uspud, French text, 133–134, and see Works
See also Letters
For the prose commentaries on the Works see p. 44 and Satie's Works
Satie, Jane, 14, 15
Satie, Jules, 13
Satie, Marguerite, 13
Satie, Olga (later Mme. Satie-Lafosse), 14, 72
Schola Cantorum, 40, 41, 43, 44, 75, 77, 116
Schönberg, 116
Schubert, 44, 54, 79

Schumann, 75
"Sea-Bird," see Satie, Adrien
Séré, O., *Musiciens français d'aujourd'hui*, 119, 142n.
Seurat, 50
S.I.M. Review, 31n. 46, 118, 135, 142, 146
Six, Les, 5 (Introduction), 52–53, 55, 59, 85, 117
Slonimsky, N. *Music since 1900*, 62n.
Smith, Sidney, 46
Société Musicale Indépendante, 41, 42, 43, 46, 111 (For Journal of, see S.I.M.)
Société Nationale, Paris, 19, 32, 42, 57, 110
Soirées de Paris, 61
Soupault, Philippe, 62, 106
Statues of Siena, 29
Strauss, Richard, 116
Stravinsky, Igor, 5 (Introduction), 41, 54, 55, 63, 87, 95, 105, 117, 118; *Mavra*, 117, 129; *Sonata for Two Pianos*, 129, illus. 129
Surrealism and Surrealists, 61, 62, 63, 101, 105, 128
Swedish Ballet, 106

Tailleferre, Germaine, 53
Taudou, 16
Templier, M. P. D., 24 and n., 38, 42n., 58
Teniers, 121
Théâtre des Champs-Elysées, 59, 64, 106
Thomas, Ambroise, 31
Time, 62 and n.
Tinchant, Albert, 24, 34, 131
Toulouse-Lautrec, 32
Tzara, Tristan, 62

Utrillo, Maurice, 126. See also p. 34

Valadon, Suzanne, 126. See also p. 34
Verdi, 119, 142
Vieux Colombier, Le, 53, 55
Viñes, Ricardo, 48, 102, 110, 111
Vinot, 14, 15, 16
Vogel, Lucien, publishers, 87
Vuillermoz, 43n., 110, 114, 140

Wagner, 18, 23, 27, 32, 54, 127, 131, 132
Wilenski, R. H., 50 and n.
"Willy," see Gauthier-Villars
Woizikovski, 102

Zürich, 62

A CATALOG OF SELECTED DOVER
BOOKS IN ALL FIELDS OF INTEREST

DRAWINGS OF REMBRANDT, edited by Seymour Slive. Updated Lippmann, Hofstede de Groot edition, with definitive scholarly apparatus. All portraits, biblical sketches, landscapes, nudes. Oriental figures, classical studies, together with selection of work by followers. 550 illustrations. Total of 630pp. 9⅛ × 12¼.
21485-0, 21486-9 Pa., Two-vol. set $29.90

GHOST AND HORROR STORIES OF AMBROSE BIERCE, Ambrose Bierce. 24 tales vividly imagined, strangely prophetic, and decades ahead of their time in technical skill: "The Damned Thing," "An Inhabitant of Carcosa," "The Eyes of the Panther," "Moxon's Master," and 20 more. 199pp. 5⅜ × 8½. 20767-6 Pa. $3.95

ETHICAL WRITINGS OF MAIMONIDES, Maimonides. Most significant ethical works of great medieval sage, newly translated for utmost precision, readability. Laws Concerning Character Traits, Eight Chapters, more. 192pp. 5⅜ × 8½.
24522-5 Pa. $4.50

THE EXPLORATION OF THE COLORADO RIVER AND ITS CANYONS, J. W. Powell. Full text of Powell's 1,000-mile expedition down the fabled Colorado in 1869. Superb account of terrain, geology, vegetation, Indians, famine, mutiny, treacherous rapids, mighty canyons, during exploration of last unknown part of continental U.S. 400pp. 5⅜ × 8½. 20094-9 Pa. $7.95

HISTORY OF PHILOSOPHY, Julián Marías. Clearest one-volume history on the market. Every major philosopher and dozens of others, to Existentialism and later. 505pp. 5⅜ × 8½. 21739-6 Pa. $9.95

ALL ABOUT LIGHTNING, Martin A. Uman. Highly readable non-technical survey of nature and causes of lightning, thunderstorms, ball lightning, St. Elmo's Fire, much more. Illustrated. 192pp. 5⅜ × 8½. 25237-X Pa. $5.95

SAILING ALONE AROUND THE WORLD, Captain Joshua Slocum. First man to sail around the world, alone, in small boat. One of great feats of seamanship told in delightful manner. 67 illustrations. 294pp. 5⅜ × 8½. 20326-3 Pa. $4.95

LETTERS AND NOTES ON THE MANNERS, CUSTOMS AND CONDITIONS OF THE NORTH AMERICAN INDIANS, George Catlin. Classic account of life among Plains Indians: ceremonies, hunt, warfare, etc. 312 plates. 572pp. of text. 6⅛ × 9¼. 22118-0, 22119-9, Pa. Two-vol. set $17.90

ALASKA: The Harriman Expedition, 1899, John Burroughs, John Muir, et al. Informative, engrossing accounts of two-month, 9,000-mile expedition. Native peoples, wildlife, forests, geography, salmon industry, glaciers, more. Profusely illustrated. 240 black-and-white line drawings. 124 black-and-white photographs. 3 maps. Index. 576pp. 5⅜ × 8½. 25109-8 Pa. $11.95

THE BOOK OF BEASTS: Being a Translation from a Latin Bestiary of the Twelfth Century, T. H. White. Wonderful catalog real and fanciful beasts: manticore, griffin, phoenix, amphivius, jaculus, many more. White's witty erudite commentary on scientific, historical aspects. Fascinating glimpse of medieval mind. Illustrated. 296pp. 5⅜ × 8¼. (Available in U.S. only) 24609-4 Pa. $6.95

FRANK LLOYD WRIGHT: ARCHITECTURE AND NATURE With 160 Illustrations, Donald Hoffmann. Profusely illustrated study of influence of nature—especially prairie—on Wright's designs for Fallingwater, Robie House, Guggenheim Museum, other masterpieces. 96pp. 9¼ × 10¾. 25098-9 Pa. $7.95

FRANK LLOYD WRIGHT'S FALLINGWATER, Donald Hoffmann. Wright's famous waterfall house: planning and construction of organic idea. History of site, owners, Wright's personal involvement. Photographs of various stages of building. Preface by Edgar Kaufmann, Jr. 100 illustrations. 112pp. 9¼ × 10.
23671-4 Pa. $8.95

YEARS WITH FRANK LLOYD WRIGHT: Apprentice to Genius, Edgar Tafel. Insightful memoir by a former apprentice presents a revealing portrait of Wright the man, the inspired teacher, the greatest American architect. 372 black-and-white illustrations. Preface. Index. vi + 228pp. 8¼ × 11. 24801-1 Pa. $10.95

THE STORY OF KING ARTHUR AND HIS KNIGHTS, Howard Pyle. Enchanting version of King Arthur fable has delighted generations with imaginative narratives of exciting adventures and unforgettable illustrations by the author. 41 illustrations. xviii + 313pp. 6⅛ × 9¼. 21445-1 Pa. $6.95

THE GODS OF THE EGYPTIANS, E. A. Wallis Budge. Thorough coverage of numerous gods of ancient Egypt by foremost Egyptologist. Information on evolution of cults, rites and gods; the cult of Osiris; the Book of the Dead and its rites; the sacred animals and birds; Heaven and Hell; and more. 956pp. 6⅛ × 9¼.
22055-9, 22056-7 Pa., Two-vol. set $21.90

A THEOLOGICO-POLITICAL TREATISE, Benedict Spinoza. Also contains unfinished *Political Treatise*. Great classic on religious liberty, theory of government on common consent. R. Elwes translation. Total of 421pp. 5⅜ × 8½.
20249-6 Pa. $6.95

INCIDENTS OF TRAVEL IN CENTRAL AMERICA, CHIAPAS, AND YUCATAN, John L. Stephens. Almost single-handed discovery of Maya culture; exploration of ruined cities, monuments, temples; customs of Indians. 115 drawings. 892pp. 5⅜ × 8½. 22404-X, 22405-8 Pa., Two-vol. set $15.90

LOS CAPRICHOS, Francisco Goya. 80 plates of wild, grotesque monsters and caricatures. Prado manuscript included. 183pp. 6⅝ × 9⅝. 22384-1 Pa. $5.95

AUTOBIOGRAPHY: The Story of My Experiments with Truth, Mohandas K. Gandhi. Not hagiography, but Gandhi in his own words. Boyhood, legal studies, purification, the growth of the Satyagraha (nonviolent protest) movement. Critical, inspiring work of the man who freed India. 480pp. 5⅜ × 8½. (Available in U.S. only)
24593-4 Pa. $6.95

ILLUSTRATED DICTIONARY OF HISTORIC ARCHITECTURE, edited by Cyril M. Harris. Extraordinary compendium of clear, concise definitions for over 5,000 important architectural terms complemented by over 2,000 line drawings. Covers full spectrum of architecture from ancient ruins to 20th-century Modernism. Preface. 592pp. 7½ × 9⅜. 24444-X Pa. $15.95

THE NIGHT BEFORE CHRISTMAS, Clement Moore. Full text, and woodcuts from original 1848 book. Also critical, historical material. 19 illustrations. 40pp. 4⅝ × 6. 22797-9 Pa. $2.50

THE LESSON OF JAPANESE ARCHITECTURE: 165 Photographs, Jiro Harada. Memorable gallery of 165 photographs taken in the 1930's of exquisite Japanese homes of the well-to-do and historic buildings. 13 line diagrams. 192pp. 8⅜ × 11¼. 24778-3 Pa. $10.95

THE AUTOBIOGRAPHY OF CHARLES DARWIN AND SELECTED LETTERS, edited by Francis Darwin. The fascinating life of eccentric genius composed of an intimate memoir by Darwin (intended for his children); commentary by his son, Francis; hundreds of fragments from notebooks, journals, papers; and letters to and from Lyell, Hooker, Huxley, Wallace and Henslow. xi + 365pp. 5⅜ × 8. 20479-0 Pa. $6.95

WONDERS OF THE SKY: Observing Rainbows, Comets, Eclipses, the Stars and Other Phenomena, Fred Schaaf. Charming, easy-to-read poetic guide to all manner of celestial events visible to the naked eye. Mock suns, glories, Belt of Venus, more. Illustrated. 299pp. 5¼ × 8¼. 24402-4 Pa. $7.95

BURNHAM'S CELESTIAL HANDBOOK, Robert Burnham, Jr. Thorough guide to the stars beyond our solar system. Exhaustive treatment. Alphabetical by constellation: Andromeda to Cetus in Vol. 1; Chamaeleon to Orion in Vol. 2; and Pavo to Vulpecula in Vol. 3. Hundreds of illustrations. Index in Vol. 3. 2,000pp. 6⅛ × 9¼. 23567-X, 23568-8, 23673-0 Pa., Three-vol. set $41.85

STAR NAMES: Their Lore and Meaning, Richard Hinckley Allen. Fascinating history of names various cultures have given to constellations and literary and folkloristic uses that have been made of stars. Indexes to subjects. Arabic and Greek names. Biblical references. Bibliography. 563pp. 5⅜ × 8½. 21079-0 Pa. $8.95

THIRTY YEARS THAT SHOOK PHYSICS: The Story of Quantum Theory, George Gamow. Lucid, accessible introduction to influential theory of energy and matter. Careful explanations of Dirac's anti-particles, Bohr's model of the atom, much more. 12 plates. Numerous drawings. 240pp. 5⅜ × 8½. 24895-X Pa. $5.95

CHINESE DOMESTIC FURNITURE IN PHOTOGRAPHS AND MEASURED DRAWINGS, Gustav Ecke. A rare volume, now affordably priced for antique collectors, furniture buffs and art historians. Detailed review of styles ranging from early Shang to late Ming. Unabridged republication. 161 black-and-white drawings, photos. Total of 224pp. 8⅜ × 11¼. (Available in U.S. only) 25171-3 Pa. $13.95

VINCENT VAN GOGH: A Biography, Julius Meier-Graefe. Dynamic, penetrating study of artist's life, relationship with brother, Theo, painting techniques, travels, more. Readable, engrossing. 160pp. 5⅜ × 8½. (Available in U.S. only) 25253-1 Pa. $4.95

HOW TO WRITE, Gertrude Stein. Gertrude Stein claimed anyone could understand her unconventional writing—here are clues to help. Fascinating improvisations, language experiments, explanations illuminate Stein's craft and the art of writing. Total of 414pp. 4⅜ × 6⅜. 23144-5 Pa. $6.95

ADVENTURES AT SEA IN THE GREAT AGE OF SAIL: Five Firsthand Narratives, edited by Elliot Snow. Rare true accounts of exploration, whaling, shipwreck, fierce natives, trade, shipboard life, more. 33 illustrations. Introduction. 353pp. 5⅜ × 8½. 25177-2 Pa. $8.95

THE HERBAL OR GENERAL HISTORY OF PLANTS, John Gerard. Classic descriptions of about 2,850 plants—with over 2,700 illustrations—includes Latin and English names, physical descriptions, varieties, time and place of growth, more. 2,706 illustrations. xlv + 1,678pp. 8½ × 12¼. 23147-X Cloth. $75.00

DOROTHY AND THE WIZARD IN OZ, L. Frank Baum. Dorothy and the Wizard visit the center of the Earth, where people are vegetables, glass houses grow and Oz characters reappear. Classic sequel to *Wizard of Oz*. 256pp. 5⅜ × 8. 24714-7 Pa. $5.95

SONGS OF EXPERIENCE: Facsimile Reproduction with 26 Plates in Full Color, William Blake. This facsimile of Blake's original "Illuminated Book" reproduces 26 full-color plates from a rare 1826 edition. Includes "The Tyger," "London," "Holy Thursday," and other immortal poems. 26 color plates. Printed text of poems. 48pp. 5¼ × 7. 24636-1 Pa. $3.50

SONGS OF INNOCENCE, William Blake. The first and most popular of Blake's famous "Illuminated Books," in a facsimile edition reproducing all 31 brightly colored plates. Additional printed text of each poem. 64pp. 5¼ × 7. 22764-2 Pa. $3.50

PRECIOUS STONES, Max Bauer. Classic, thorough study of diamonds, rubies, emeralds, garnets, etc.: physical character, occurrence, properties, use, similar topics. 20 plates, 8 in color. 94 figures. 659pp. 6⅛ × 9¼. 21910-0, 21911-9 Pa., Two-vol. set $15.90

ENCYCLOPEDIA OF VICTORIAN NEEDLEWORK, S. F. A. Caulfeild and Blanche Saward. Full, precise descriptions of stitches, techniques for dozens of needlecrafts—most exhaustive reference of its kind. Over 800 figures. Total of 679pp. 8⅛ × 11. Two volumes. Vol. 1 22800-2 Pa. $11.95
Vol. 2 22801-0 Pa. $11.95

THE MARVELOUS LAND OF OZ, L. Frank Baum. Second Oz book, the Scarecrow and Tin Woodman are back with hero named Tip, Oz magic. 136 illustrations. 287pp. 5⅜ × 8½. 20692-0 Pa. $5.95

WILD FOWL DECOYS, Joel Barber. Basic book on the subject, by foremost authority and collector. Reveals history of decoy making and rigging, place in American culture, different kinds of decoys, how to make them, and how to use them. 140 plates. 156pp. 7⅞ × 10¾. 20011-6 Pa. $8.95

HISTORY OF LACE, Mrs. Bury Palliser. Definitive, profusely illustrated chronicle of lace from earliest times to late 19th century. Laces of Italy, Greece, England, France, Belgium, etc. Landmark of needlework scholarship. 266 illustrations. 672pp. 6⅛ × 9¼. 24742-2 Pa. $14.95

ILLUSTRATED GUIDE TO SHAKER FURNITURE, Robert Meader. All furniture and appurtenances, with much on unknown local styles. 235 photos. 146pp. 9 × 12. 22819-3 Pa. $8.95

WHALE SHIPS AND WHALING: A Pictorial Survey, George Francis Dow. Over 200 vintage engravings, drawings, photographs of barks, brigs, cutters, other vessels. Also harpoons, lances, whaling guns, many other artifacts. Comprehensive text by foremost authority. 207 black-and-white illustrations. 288pp. 6 × 9. 24808-9 Pa. $8.95

THE BERTRAMS, Anthony Trollope. Powerful portrayal of blind self-will and thwarted ambition includes one of Trollope's most heartrending love stories. 497pp. 5⅜ × 8½. 25119-5 Pa. $9.95

ADVENTURES WITH A HAND LENS, Richard Headstrom. Clearly written guide to observing and studying flowers and grasses, fish scales, moth and insect wings, egg cases, buds, feathers, seeds, leaf scars, moss, molds, ferns, common crystals, etc.—all with an ordinary, inexpensive magnifying glass. 209 exact line drawings aid in your discoveries. 220pp. 5⅜ × 8½. 23330-8 Pa. $4.95

RODIN ON ART AND ARTISTS, Auguste Rodin. Great sculptor's candid, wide-ranging comments on meaning of art; great artists; relation of sculpture to poetry, painting, music; philosophy of life, more. 76 superb black-and-white illustrations of Rodin's sculpture, drawings and prints. 119pp. 8⅜ × 11¼. 24487-3 Pa. $7.95

FIFTY CLASSIC FRENCH FILMS, 1912–1982: A Pictorial Record, Anthony Slide. Memorable stills from Grand Illusion, Beauty and the Beast, Hiroshima, Mon Amour, many more. Credits, plot synopses, reviews, etc. 160pp. 8¼ × 11. 25256-6 Pa. $11.95

THE PRINCIPLES OF PSYCHOLOGY, William James. Famous long course complete, unabridged. Stream of thought, time perception, memory, experimental methods; great work decades ahead of its time. 94 figures. 1,391pp. 5⅜ × 8½. 20381-6, 20382-4 Pa., Two-vol. set $23.90

BODIES IN A BOOKSHOP, R. T. Campbell. Challenging mystery of blackmail and murder with ingenious plot and superbly drawn characters. In the best tradition of British suspense fiction. 192pp. 5⅜ × 8½. 24720-1 Pa. $3.95

CALLAS: PORTRAIT OF A PRIMA DONNA, George Jellinek. Renowned commentator on the musical scene chronicles incredible career and life of the most controversial, fascinating, influential operatic personality of our time. 64 black-and-white photographs. 416pp. 5⅜ × 8¼. 25047-4 Pa. $8.95

GEOMETRY, RELATIVITY AND THE FOURTH DIMENSION, Rudolph Rucker. Exposition of fourth dimension, concepts of relativity as Flatland characters continue adventures. Popular, easily followed yet accurate, profound. 141 illustrations. 133pp. 5⅜ × 8½. 23400-2 Pa. $4.95

HOUSEHOLD STORIES BY THE BROTHERS GRIMM, with pictures by Walter Crane. 53 classic stories—Rumpelstiltskin, Rapunzel, Hansel and Gretel, the Fisherman and his Wife, Snow White, Tom Thumb, Sleeping Beauty, Cinderella, and so much more—lavishly illustrated with original 19th century drawings. 114 illustrations. x + 269pp. 5⅜ × 8½. 21080-4 Pa. $4.95

SUNDIALS, Albert Waugh. Far and away the best, most thorough coverage of ideas, mathematics concerned, types, construction, adjusting anywhere. Over 100 illustrations. 230pp. 5⅜ × 8½. 22947-5 Pa. $4.95

PICTURE HISTORY OF THE NORMANDIE: With 190 Illustrations, Frank O. Braynard. Full story of legendary French ocean liner: Art Deco interiors, design innovations, furnishings, celebrities, maiden voyage, tragic fire, much more. Extensive text. 144pp. 8⅞ × 11¾. 25257-4 Pa. $10.95

THE FIRST AMERICAN COOKBOOK: A Facsimile of "American Cookery," 1796, Amelia Simmons. Facsimile of the first American-written cookbook published in the United States contains authentic recipes for colonial favorites—pumpkin pudding, winter squash pudding, spruce beer, Indian slapjacks, and more. Introductory Essay and Glossary of colonial cooking terms. 80pp. 5⅜ × 8½. 24710-4 Pa. $3.50

101 PUZZLES IN THOUGHT AND LOGIC, C. R. Wylie, Jr. Solve murders and robberies, find out which fishermen are liars, how a blind man could possibly identify a color—purely by your own reasoning! 107pp. 5⅜ × 8½. 20367-0 Pa. $2.50

THE BOOK OF WORLD-FAMOUS MUSIC—CLASSICAL, POPULAR AND FOLK, James J. Fuld. Revised and enlarged republication of landmark work in musico-bibliography. Full information about nearly 1,000 songs and compositions including first lines of music and lyrics. New supplement. Index. 800pp. 5⅜ × 8¼. 24857-7 Pa. $15.95

ANTHROPOLOGY AND MODERN LIFE, Franz Boas. Great anthropologist's classic treatise on race and culture. Introduction by Ruth Bunzel. Only inexpensive paperback edition. 255pp. 5⅜ × 8½. 25245-0 Pa. $6.95

THE TALE OF PETER RABBIT, Beatrix Potter. The inimitable Peter's terrifying adventure in Mr. McGregor's garden, with all 27 wonderful, full-color Potter illustrations. 55pp. 4¼ × 5½. (Available in U.S. only) 22827-4 Pa. $1.75

THREE PROPHETIC SCIENCE FICTION NOVELS, H. G. Wells. *When the Sleeper Wakes, A Story of the Days to Come* and *The Time Machine* (full version). 335pp. 5⅜ × 8½. (Available in U.S. only) 20605-X Pa. $6.95

APICIUS COOKERY AND DINING IN IMPERIAL ROME, edited and translated by Joseph Dommers Vehling. Oldest known cookbook in existence offers readers a clear picture of what foods Romans ate, how they prepared them, etc. 49 illustrations. 301pp. 6⅛ × 9¼. 23563-7 Pa. $7.95

SHAKESPEARE LEXICON AND QUOTATION DICTIONARY, Alexander Schmidt. Full definitions, locations, shades of meaning of every word in plays and poems. More than 50,000 exact quotations. 1,485pp. 6½ × 9¼. 22726-X, 22727-8 Pa., Two-vol. set $29.90

THE WORLD'S GREAT SPEECHES, edited by Lewis Copeland and Lawrence W. Lamm. Vast collection of 278 speeches from Greeks to 1970. Powerful and effective models; unique look at history. 842pp. 5⅜ × 8½. 20468-5 Pa. $11.95

THE BLUE FAIRY BOOK, Andrew Lang. The first, most famous collection, with many familiar tales: Little Red Riding Hood, Aladdin and the Wonderful Lamp, Puss in Boots, Sleeping Beauty, Hansel and Gretel, Rumpelstiltskin; 37 in all. 138 illustrations. 390pp. 5⅜ × 8½. 21437-0 Pa. $6.95

THE STORY OF THE CHAMPIONS OF THE ROUND TABLE, Howard Pyle. Sir Launcelot, Sir Tristram and Sir Percival in spirited adventures of love and triumph retold in Pyle's inimitable style. 50 drawings, 31 full-page. xviii + 329pp. 6½ × 9¼. 21883-X Pa. $7.95

AUDUBON AND HIS JOURNALS, Maria Audubon. Unmatched two-volume portrait of the great artist, naturalist and author contains his journals, an excellent biography by his granddaughter, expert annotations by the noted ornithologist, Dr. Elliott Coues, and 37 superb illustrations. Total of 1,200pp. 5⅜ × 8.
Vol. I 25143-8 Pa. $8.95
Vol. II 25144-6 Pa. $8.95

GREAT DINOSAUR HUNTERS AND THEIR DISCOVERIES, Edwin H. Colbert. Fascinating, lavishly illustrated chronicle of dinosaur research, 1820's to 1960. Achievements of Cope, Marsh, Brown, Buckland, Mantell, Huxley, many others. 384pp. 5¼ × 8¼. 24701-5 Pa. $7.95

THE TASTEMAKERS, Russell Lynes. Informal, illustrated social history of American taste 1850's-1950's. First popularized categories Highbrow, Lowbrow, Middlebrow. 129 illustrations. New (1979) afterword. 384pp. 6 × 9.
23993-4 Pa. $8.95

DOUBLE CROSS PURPOSES, Ronald A. Knox. A treasure hunt in the Scottish Highlands, an old map, unidentified corpse, surprise discoveries keep reader guessing in this cleverly intricate tale of financial skullduggery. 2 black-and-white maps. 320pp. 5⅜ × 8½. (Available in U.S. only) 25032-6 Pa. $6.95

AUTHENTIC VICTORIAN DECORATION AND ORNAMENTATION IN FULL COLOR: 46 Plates from "Studies in Design," Christopher Dresser. Superb full-color lithographs reproduced from rare original portfolio of a major Victorian designer. 48pp. 9¼ × 12¼. 25083-0 Pa. $7.95

PRIMITIVE ART, Franz Boas. Remains the best text ever prepared on subject, thoroughly discussing Indian, African, Asian, Australian, and, especially, Northern American primitive art. Over 950 illustrations show ceramics, masks, totem poles, weapons, textiles, paintings, much more. 376pp. 5⅜ × 8. 20025-6 Pa. $7.95

SIDELIGHTS ON RELATIVITY, Albert Einstein. Unabridged republication of two lectures delivered by the great physicist in 1920-21. *Ether and Relativity* and *Geometry and Experience*. Elegant ideas in non-mathematical form, accessible to intelligent layman. vi + 56pp. 5⅜ × 8½. 24511-X Pa. $2.95

THE WIT AND HUMOR OF OSCAR WILDE, edited by Alvin Redman. More than 1,000 ripostes, paradoxes, wisecracks: Work is the curse of the drinking classes, I can resist everything except temptation, etc. 258pp. 5⅜ × 8½. 20602-5 Pa. $4.95

ADVENTURES WITH A MICROSCOPE, Richard Headstrom. 59 adventures with clothing fibers, protozoa, ferns and lichens, roots and leaves, much more. 142 illustrations. 232pp. 5⅜ × 8½. 23471-1 Pa. $3.95

PLANTS OF THE BIBLE, Harold N. Moldenke and Alma L. Moldenke. Standard reference to all 230 plants mentioned in Scriptures. Latin name, biblical reference, uses, modern identity, much more. Unsurpassed encyclopedic resource for scholars, botanists, nature lovers, students of Bible. Bibliography. Indexes. 123 black-and-white illustrations. 384pp. 6 × 9. 25069-5 Pa. $8.95

FAMOUS AMERICAN WOMEN: A Biographical Dictionary from Colonial Times to the Present, Robert McHenry, ed. From Pocahontas to Rosa Parks, 1,035 distinguished American women documented in separate biographical entries. Accurate, up-to-date data, numerous categories, spans 400 years. Indices. 493pp. 6½ × 9¼. 24523-3 Pa. $10.95

THE FABULOUS INTERIORS OF THE GREAT OCEAN LINERS IN HISTORIC PHOTOGRAPHS, William H. Miller, Jr. Some 200 superb photographs capture exquisite interiors of world's great "floating palaces"—1890's to 1980's: *Titanic, Ile de France, Queen Elizabeth, United States, Europa,* more. Approx. 200 black-and-white photographs. Captions. Text. Introduction. 160pp. 8⅞ × 11¾. 24756-2 Pa. $9.95

THE GREAT LUXURY LINERS, 1927–1954: A Photographic Record, William H. Miller, Jr. Nostalgic tribute to heyday of ocean liners. 186 photos of Ile de France, Normandie, Leviathan, Queen Elizabeth, United States, many others. Interior and exterior views. Introduction. Captions. 160pp. 9 × 12. 24056-8 Pa. $10.95

A NATURAL HISTORY OF THE DUCKS, John Charles Phillips. Great landmark of ornithology offers complete detailed coverage of nearly 200 species and subspecies of ducks: gadwall, sheldrake, merganser, pintail, many more. 74 full-color plates, 102 black-and-white. Bibliography. Total of 1,920pp. 8⅜ × 11¼. 25141-1, 25142-X Cloth. Two-vol. set $100.00

THE SEAWEED HANDBOOK: An Illustrated Guide to Seaweeds from North Carolina to Canada, Thomas F. Lee. Concise reference covers 78 species. Scientific and common names, habitat, distribution, more. Finding keys for easy identification. 224pp. 5⅜ × 8½. 25215-9 Pa. $6.95

THE TEN BOOKS OF ARCHITECTURE: The 1755 Leoni Edition, Leon Battista Alberti. Rare classic helped introduce the glories of ancient architecture to the Renaissance. 68 black-and-white plates. 336pp. 8⅜ × 11¼. 25239-6 Pa. $14.95

MISS MACKENZIE, Anthony Trollope. Minor masterpieces by Victorian master unmasks many truths about life in 19th-century England. First inexpensive edition in years. 392pp. 5⅜ × 8½. 25201-9 Pa. $8.95

THE RIME OF THE ANCIENT MARINER, Gustave Doré, Samuel Taylor Coleridge. Dramatic engravings considered by many to be his greatest work. The terrifying space of the open sea, the storms and whirlpools of an unknown ocean, the ice of Antarctica, more—all rendered in a powerful, chilling manner. Full text. 38 plates. 77pp. 9¼ × 12. 22305-1 Pa. $4.95

THE EXPEDITIONS OF ZEBULON MONTGOMERY PIKE, Zebulon Montgomery Pike. Fascinating first-hand accounts (1805–6) of exploration of Mississippi River, Indian wars, capture by Spanish dragoons, much more. 1,088pp. 5⅜ × 8½. 25254-X, 25255-8 Pa. Two-vol. set $25.90

CATALOG OF DOVER BOOKS

A CONCISE HISTORY OF PHOTOGRAPHY: Third Revised Edition, Helmut Gernsheim. Best one-volume history—camera obscura, photochemistry, daguerreotypes, evolution of cameras, film, more. Also artistic aspects—landscape, portraits, fine art, etc. 281 black-and-white photographs. 26 in color. 176pp. 8⅜ × 11¼. 25128-4 Pa. $13.95

THE DORÉ BIBLE ILLUSTRATIONS, Gustave Doré. 241 detailed plates from the Bible: the Creation scenes, Adam and Eve, Flood, Babylon, battle sequences, life of Jesus, etc. Each plate is accompanied by the verses from the King James version of the Bible. 241pp. 9 × 12. 23004-X Pa. $9.95

HUGGER-MUGGER IN THE LOUVRE, Elliot Paul. Second Homer Evans mystery-comedy. Theft at the Louvre involves sleuth in hilarious, madcap caper. "A knockout."—Books. 336pp. 5⅜ × 8½. 25185-3 Pa. $5.95

FLATLAND, E. A. Abbott. Intriguing and enormously popular science-fiction classic explores the complexities of trying to survive as a two-dimensional being in a three-dimensional world. Amusingly illustrated by the author. 16 illustrations. 103pp. 5⅜ × 8½. 20001-9 Pa. $2.50

THE HISTORY OF THE LEWIS AND CLARK EXPEDITION, Meriwether Lewis and William Clark, edited by Elliott Coues. Classic edition of Lewis and Clark's day-by-day journals that later became the basis for U.S. claims to Oregon and the West. Accurate and invaluable geographical, botanical, biological, meteorological and anthropological material. Total of 1,508pp. 5⅜ × 8½. 21268-8, 21269-6, 21270-X Pa. Three-vol. set $26.85

LANGUAGE, TRUTH AND LOGIC, Alfred J. Ayer. Famous, clear introduction to Vienna, Cambridge schools of Logical Positivism. Role of philosophy, elimination of metaphysics, nature of analysis, etc. 160pp. 5⅜ × 8½. (Available in U.S. and Canada only) 20010-8 Pa. $3.95

MATHEMATICS FOR THE NONMATHEMATICIAN, Morris Kline. Detailed, college-level treatment of mathematics in cultural and historical context, with numerous exercises. For liberal arts students. Preface. Recommended Reading Lists. Tables. Index. Numerous black-and-white figures. xvi + 641pp. 5⅜ × 8½. 24823-2 Pa. $11.95

HANDBOOK OF PICTORIAL SYMBOLS, Rudolph Modley. 3,250 signs and symbols, many systems in full; official or heavy commercial use. Arranged by subject. Most in Pictorial Archive series. 143pp. 8⅛ × 11. 23357-X Pa. $6.95

INCIDENTS OF TRAVEL IN YUCATAN, John L. Stephens. Classic (1843) exploration of jungles of Yucatan, looking for evidences of Maya civilization. Travel adventures, Mexican and Indian culture, etc. Total of 669pp. 5⅜ × 8½. 20926-1, 20927-X Pa., Two-vol. set $11.90

DEGAS: An Intimate Portrait, Ambroise Vollard. Charming, anecdotal memoir by famous art dealer of one of the greatest 19th-century French painters. 14 black-and-white illustrations. Introduction by Harold L. Van Doren. 96pp. 5⅜ × 8½.
25131-4 Pa. $4.95

PERSONAL NARRATIVE OF A PILGRIMAGE TO ALMANDINAH AND MECCAH, Richard Burton. Great travel classic by remarkably colorful personality. Burton, disguised as a Moroccan, visited sacred shrines of Islam, narrowly escaping death. 47 illustrations. 959pp. 5⅜ × 8½. 21217-3, 21218-1 Pa., Two-vol. set $19.90

PHRASE AND WORD ORIGINS, A. H. Holt. Entertaining, reliable, modern study of more than 1,200 colorful words, phrases, origins and histories. Much unexpected information. 254pp. 5⅜ × 8½.
20758-7 Pa. $5.95

THE RED THUMB MARK, R. Austin Freeman. In this first Dr. Thorndyke case, the great scientific detective draws fascinating conclusions from the nature of a single fingerprint. Exciting story, authentic science. 320pp. 5⅜ × 8½. (Available in U.S. only)
25210-8 Pa. $6.95

AN EGYPTIAN HIEROGLYPHIC DICTIONARY, E. A. Wallis Budge. Monumental work containing about 25,000 words or terms that occur in texts ranging from 3000 B.C. to 600 A.D. Each entry consists of a transliteration of the word, the word in hieroglyphs, and the meaning in English. 1,314pp. 6⅜ × 10.
23615-3, 23616-1 Pa., Two-vol. set $31.90

THE COMPLEAT STRATEGYST: Being a Primer on the Theory of Games of Strategy, J. D. Williams. Highly entertaining classic describes, with many illustrated examples, how to select best strategies in conflict situations. Prefaces. Appendices. xvi + 268pp. 5⅜ × 8½.
25101-2 Pa. $5.95

THE ROAD TO OZ, L. Frank Baum. Dorothy meets the Shaggy Man, little Button-Bright and the Rainbow's beautiful daughter in this delightful trip to the magical Land of Oz. 272pp. 5⅜ × 8.
25208-6 Pa. $5.95

POINT AND LINE TO PLANE, Wassily Kandinsky. Seminal exposition of role of point, line, other elements in non-objective painting. Essential to understanding 20th-century art. 127 illustrations. 192pp. 6½ × 9¼.
23808-3 Pa. $5.95

LADY ANNA, Anthony Trollope. Moving chronicle of Countess Lovel's bitter struggle to win for herself and daughter Anna their rightful rank and fortune— perhaps at cost of sanity itself. 384pp. 5⅜ × 8½.
24669-8 Pa. $8.95

EGYPTIAN MAGIC, E. A. Wallis Budge. Sums up all that is known about magic in Ancient Egypt: the role of magic in controlling the gods, powerful amulets that warded off evil spirits, scarabs of immortality, use of wax images, formulas and spells, the secret name, much more. 253pp. 5⅜ × 8½.
22681-6 Pa. $4.50

THE DANCE OF SIVA, Ananda Coomaraswamy. Preeminent authority unfolds the vast metaphysic of India: the revelation of her art, conception of the universe, social organization, etc. 27 reproductions of art masterpieces. 192pp. 5⅜ × 8½.
24817-8 Pa. $5.95

CHRISTMAS CUSTOMS AND TRADITIONS, Clement A. Miles. Origin, evolution, significance of religious, secular practices. Caroling, gifts, yule logs, much more. Full, scholarly yet fascinating; non-sectarian. 400pp. 5⅜ × 8½.
23354-5 Pa. $6.95

THE HUMAN FIGURE IN MOTION, Eadweard Muybridge. More than 4,500 stopped-action photos, in action series, showing undraped men, women, children jumping, lying down, throwing, sitting, wrestling, carrying, etc. 390pp. 7⅞ × 10⅝.
20204-6 Cloth. $21.95

THE MAN WHO WAS THURSDAY, Gilbert Keith Chesterton. Witty, fast-paced novel about a club of anarchists in turn-of-the-century London. Brilliant social, religious, philosophical speculations. 128pp. 5⅜ × 8½.
25121-7 Pa. $3.95

A CEZANNE SKETCHBOOK: Figures, Portraits, Landscapes and Still Lifes, Paul Cezanne. Great artist experiments with tonal effects, light, mass, other qualities in over 100 drawings. A revealing view of developing master painter, precursor of Cubism. 102 black-and-white illustrations. 144pp. 8¾ × 6⅝.
24790-2 Pa. $5.95

AN ENCYCLOPEDIA OF BATTLES: Accounts of Over 1,560 Battles from 1479 B.C. to the Present, David Eggenberger. Presents essential details of every major battle in recorded history, from the first battle of Megiddo in 1479 B.C. to Grenada in 1984. List of Battle Maps. New Appendix covering the years 1967–1984. Index. 99 illustrations. 544pp. 6½ × 9¼.
24913-1 Pa. $14.95

AN ETYMOLOGICAL DICTIONARY OF MODERN ENGLISH, Ernest Weekley. Richest, fullest work, by foremost British lexicographer. Detailed word histories. Inexhaustible. Total of 856pp. 6½ × 9¼.
21873-2, 21874-0 Pa., Two-vol. set $17.00

WEBSTER'S AMERICAN MILITARY BIOGRAPHIES, edited by Robert McHenry. Over 1,000 figures who shaped 3 centuries of American military history. Detailed biographies of Nathan Hale, Douglas MacArthur, Mary Hallaren, others. Chronologies of engagements, more. Introduction. Addenda. 1,033 entries in alphabetical order. xi + 548pp. 6½ × 9¼. (Available in U.S. only)
24758-9 Pa. $13.95

LIFE IN ANCIENT EGYPT, Adolf Erman. Detailed older account, with much not in more recent books: domestic life, religion, magic, medicine, commerce, and whatever else needed for complete picture. Many illustrations. 597pp. 5⅜ × 8½.
22632-8 Pa. $8.95

HISTORIC COSTUME IN PICTURES, Braun & Schneider. Over 1,450 costumed figures shown, covering a wide variety of peoples: kings, emperors, nobles, priests, servants, soldiers, scholars, townsfolk, peasants, merchants, courtiers, cavaliers, and more. 256pp. 8⅜ × 11¼.
23150-X Pa. $9.95

THE NOTEBOOKS OF LEONARDO DA VINCI, edited by J. P. Richter. Extracts from manuscripts reveal great genius; on painting, sculpture, anatomy, sciences, geography, etc. Both Italian and English. 186 ms. pages reproduced, plus 500 additional drawings, including studies for *Last Supper, Sforza* monument, etc. 860pp. 7⅞ × 10¾. (Available in U.S. only) 22572-0, 22573-9 Pa., Two-vol. set $31.90

CATALOG OF DOVER BOOKS

THE ART NOUVEAU STYLE BOOK OF ALPHONSE MUCHA: All 72 Plates from "Documents Decoratifs" in Original Color, Alphonse Mucha. Rare copyright-free design portfolio by high priest of Art Nouveau. Jewelry, wallpaper, stained glass, furniture, figure studies, plant and animal motifs, etc. Only complete one-volume edition. 80pp. 9⅜ × 12¼. 24044-4 Pa. $9.95

ANIMALS: 1,419 COPYRIGHT-FREE ILLUSTRATIONS OF MAMMALS, BIRDS, FISH, INSECTS, ETC., edited by Jim Harter. Clear wood engravings present, in extremely lifelike poses, over 1,000 species of animals. One of the most extensive pictorial sourcebooks of its kind. Captions. Index. 284pp. 9 × 12. 23766-4 Pa. $9.95

OBELISTS FLY HIGH, C. Daly King. Masterpiece of American detective fiction, long out of print, involves murder on a 1935 transcontinental flight—"a very thrilling story"—NY Times. Unabridged and unaltered republication of the edition published by William Collins Sons & Co. Ltd., London, 1935. 288pp. 5⅜ × 8½. (Available in U.S. only) 25036-9 Pa. $5.95

VICTORIAN AND EDWARDIAN FASHION: A Photographic Survey, Alison Gernsheim. First fashion history completely illustrated by contemporary photographs. Full text plus 235 photos, 1840–1914, in which many celebrities appear. 240pp. 6½ × 9¼. 24205-6 Pa. $6.95

THE ART OF THE FRENCH ILLUSTRATED BOOK, 1700–1914, Gordon N. Ray. Over 630 superb book illustrations by Fragonard, Delacroix, Daumier, Doré, Grandville, Manet, Mucha, Steinlen, Toulouse-Lautrec and many others. Preface. Introduction. 633 halftones. Indices of artists, authors & titles, binders and provenances. Appendices. Bibliography. 608pp. 8⅜ × 11¼. 25086-5 Pa. $24.95

THE WONDERFUL WIZARD OF OZ, L. Frank Baum. Facsimile in full color of America's finest children's classic. 143 illustrations by W. W. Denslow. 267pp. 5⅜ × 8½. 20691-2 Pa. $7.95

FRONTIERS OF MODERN PHYSICS: New Perspectives on Cosmology, Relativity, Black Holes and Extraterrestrial Intelligence, Tony Rothman, et al. For the intelligent layman. Subjects include: cosmological models of the universe; black holes; the neutrino; the search for extraterrestrial intelligence. Introduction. 46 black-and-white illustrations. 192pp. 5⅜ × 8½. 24587-X Pa. $7.95

THE FRIENDLY STARS, Martha Evans Martin & Donald Howard Menzel. Classic text marshalls the stars together in an engaging, non-technical survey, presenting them as sources of beauty in night sky. 23 illustrations. Foreword. 2 star charts. Index. 147pp. 5⅜ × 8½. 21099-5 Pa. $3.95

FADS AND FALLACIES IN THE NAME OF SCIENCE, Martin Gardner. Fair, witty appraisal of cranks, quacks, and quackeries of science and pseudoscience: hollow earth, Velikovsky, orgone energy, Dianetics, flying saucers, Bridey Murphy, food and medical fads, etc. Revised, expanded In the Name of Science. "A very able and even-tempered presentation."—The New Yorker. 363pp. 5⅜ × 8. 20394-8 Pa. $6.95

ANCIENT EGYPT: ITS CULTURE AND HISTORY, J. E Manchip White. From pre-dynastics through Ptolemies: society, history, political structure, religion, daily life, literature, cultural heritage. 48 plates. 217pp. 5⅜ × 8½. 22548-8 Pa. $5.95

CATALOG OF DOVER BOOKS

SIR HARRY HOTSPUR OF HUMBLETHWAITE, Anthony Trollope. Incisive, unconventional psychological study of a conflict between a wealthy baronet, his idealistic daughter, and their scapegrace cousin. The 1870 novel in its first inexpensive edition in years. 250pp. 5⅜ × 8½. 24953-0 Pa. $5.95

LASERS AND HOLOGRAPHY, Winston E. Kock. Sound introduction to burgeoning field, expanded (1981) for second edition. Wave patterns, coherence, lasers, diffraction, zone plates, properties of holograms, recent advances. 84 illustrations. 160pp. 5⅜ × 8¼. (Except in United Kingdom) 24041-X Pa. $3.95

INTRODUCTION TO ARTIFICIAL INTELLIGENCE: SECOND, ENLARGED EDITION, Philip C. Jackson, Jr. Comprehensive survey of artificial intelligence—the study of how machines (computers) can be made to act intelligently. Includes introductory and advanced material. Extensive notes updating the main text. 132 black-and-white illustrations. 512pp. 5⅜ × 8½. 24864-X Pa. $8.95

HISTORY OF INDIAN AND INDONESIAN ART, Ananda K. Coomaraswamy. Over 400 illustrations illuminate classic study of Indian art from earliest Harappa finds to early 20th century. Provides philosophical, religious and social insights. 304pp. 6⅜ × 9⅜. 25005-9 Pa. $9.95

THE GOLEM, Gustav Meyrink. Most famous supernatural novel in modern European literature, set in Ghetto of Old Prague around 1890. Compelling story of mystical experiences, strange transformations, profound terror. 13 black-and-white illustrations. 224pp. 5⅜ × 8½. (Available in U.S. only) 25025-3 Pa. $6.95

PICTORIAL ENCYCLOPEDIA OF HISTORIC ARCHITECTURAL PLANS, DETAILS AND ELEMENTS: With 1,880 Line Drawings of Arches, Domes, Doorways, Facades, Gables, Windows, etc., John Theodore Haneman. Sourcebook of inspiration for architects, designers, others. Bibliography. Captions. 141pp. 9 × 12. 24605-1 Pa. $7.95

BENCHLEY LOST AND FOUND, Robert Benchley. Finest humor from early 30's, about pet peeves, child psychologists, post office and others. Mostly unavailable elsewhere. 73 illustrations by Peter Arno and others. 183pp. 5⅜ × 8½. 22410-4 Pa. $4.95

ERTÉ GRAPHICS, Erté. Collection of striking color graphics: Seasons, Alphabet, Numerals, Aces and Precious Stones. 50 plates, including 4 on covers. 48pp. 9⅜ × 12¼. 23580-7 Pa. $7.95

THE JOURNAL OF HENRY D. THOREAU, edited by Bradford Torrey, F. H. Allen. Complete reprinting of 14 volumes, 1837–61, over two million words; the sourcebooks for Walden, etc. Definitive. All original sketches, plus 75 photographs. 1,804pp. 8½ × 12¼. 20312-3, 20313-1 Cloth., Two-vol. set $120.00

CASTLES: THEIR CONSTRUCTION AND HISTORY, Sidney Toy. Traces castle development from ancient roots. Nearly 200 photographs and drawings illustrate moats, keeps, baileys, many other features. Caernarvon, Dover Castles, Hadrian's Wall, Tower of London, dozens more. 256pp. 5⅜ × 8¼. 24898-4 Pa. $6.95

CATALOG OF DOVER BOOKS

AMERICAN CLIPPER SHIPS: 1833–1858, Octavius T. Howe & Frederick C. Matthews. Fully-illustrated, encyclopedic review of 352 clipper ships from the period of America's greatest maritime supremacy. Introduction. 109 halftones. 5 black-and-white line illustrations. Index. Total of 928pp. 5⅜ × 8½.
25115-2, 25116-0 Pa., Two-vol. set $17.90

TOWARDS A NEW ARCHITECTURE, Le Corbusier. Pioneering manifesto by great architect, near legendary founder of "International School." Technical and aesthetic theories, views on industry, economics, relation of form to function, "mass-production spirit," much more. Profusely illustrated. Unabridged translation of 13th French edition. Introduction by Frederick Etchells. 320pp. 6⅛ × 9¼.
(Available in U.S. only) 25023-7 Pa. $8.95

THE BOOK OF KELLS, edited by Blanche Cirker. Inexpensive collection of 32 full-color, full-page plates from the greatest illuminated manuscript of the Middle Ages, painstakingly reproduced from rare facsimile edition. Publisher's Note. Captions. 32pp. 9⅜ × 12¼. 24345-1 Pa. $4.95

BEST SCIENCE FICTION STORIES OF H. G. WELLS, H. G. Wells. Full novel *The Invisible Man*, plus 17 short stories: "The Crystal Egg," "Aepyornis Island," "The Strange Orchid," etc. 303pp. 5⅜ × 8½. (Available in U.S. only)
21531-8 Pa. $6.95

AMERICAN SAILING SHIPS: Their Plans and History, Charles G. Davis. Photos, construction details of schooners, frigates, clippers, other sailcraft of 18th to early 20th centuries—plus entertaining discourse on design, rigging, nautical lore, much more. 137 black-and-white illustrations. 240pp. 6⅛ × 9¼.
24658-2 Pa. $6.95

ENTERTAINING MATHEMATICAL PUZZLES, Martin Gardner. Selection of author's favorite conundrums involving arithmetic, money, speed, etc., with lively commentary. Complete solutions. 112pp. 5⅜ × 8½. 25211-6 Pa. $2.95

THE WILL TO BELIEVE, HUMAN IMMORTALITY, William James. Two books bound together. Effect of irrational on logical, and arguments for human immortality. 402pp. 5⅜ × 8½. 20291-7 Pa. $7.95

THE HAUNTED MONASTERY and THE CHINESE MAZE MURDERS, Robert Van Gulik. 2 full novels by Van Gulik continue adventures of Judge Dee and his companions. An evil Taoist monastery, seemingly supernatural events; overgrown topiary maze that hides strange crimes. Set in 7th-century China. 27 illustrations. 328pp. 5⅜ × 8½. 23502-5 Pa. $6.95

CELEBRATED CASES OF JUDGE DEE (DEE GOONG AN), translated by Robert Van Gulik. Authentic 18th-century Chinese detective novel; Dee and associates solve three interlocked cases. Led to Van Gulik's own stories with same characters. Extensive introduction. 9 illustrations. 237pp. 5⅜ × 8½.
23337-5 Pa. $4.95

Prices subject to change without notice.
Available at your book dealer or write for free catalog to Dept. GI, Dover Publications, Inc., 31 East 2nd St., Mineola, N.Y. 11501. Dover publishes more than 175 books each year on science, elementary and advanced mathematics, biology, music, art, literary history, social sciences and other areas.
